ULTIMATE DINOSAURS
ANKYLOSAURUS

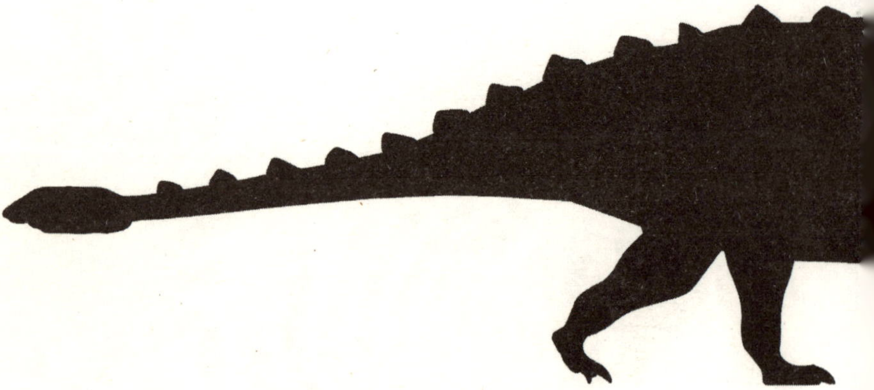

BEN GARROD

ULTIMATE DINOSAURS
ANKYLOSAURUS

ZEPHYR
An imprint of Head of Zeus

This is a Zephyr book, first published in the UK in 2023 at Head of Zeus,
part of Bloomsbury Publishing Plc

Text © Ben Garrod, 2023

Palaeo Art © Scott Hartman, 2023, and Gabriel Ugueto, 2023

Cartoon illustrations © Ethan Kocak, 2023

The moral right of Ben Garrod to be identified as the author and of Scott Hartman, Gabriel Ugueto and Ethan Kocak to be identified as the artists of this work have been asserted in accordance with the Copyright, Designs and Patents Act of 1988.

All rights reserved. No part of this publication may be reproduced, stored in a retrieval system, or transmitted in any form or by any means, electronic, mechanical, photocopying, recording, or otherwise, without the prior permission of both the copyright owner and the above publisher of this book.

9 8 7 6 5 4 3 2 1

A CIP catalogue record for this book is available from the British Library.

ISBN (PB): 9781804548271
ISBN (E): 9781804548257

Designed by Nicky Borowiec

Printed and bound in Great Britain
by CPI Group (UK) Ltd, Croydon CR0 4YY

MIX
Paper | Supporting
responsible forestry
FSC® C171272

Head of Zeus
5–8 Hardwick Street
London EC1R 4RG

WWW.HEADOFZEUS.COM

For geeky scientists

who are super-heroes too

1 DINOSAUR DEFINITIONS   15
What *is* a Dinosaur?
Definitely Dinosaurs
Dino Checklist

2 DINOSAUR DETECTIVES   27
Ankylosaurus
Family Tree
Ankylosaurus Relatives

3 DINOSAUR DISCOVERIES   41
When and Where

ASK AN EXPERT: WOULD DINOSAURS MAKE GOOD PETS?   47

CONTENTS

4 DELVE INTO A DINOSAUR 53
Anatomy of *Ankylosaurus*

The Skeleton

The Body

5 DINOSAUR DOMAINS 69
Habitats and Ecosystems

NEW SCIENCE: HOW *ANKYLOSAURUS* GOT ITS TAIL 75

6 DODGING DINOSAURS 83
Evolutionary Arms Race

The Battle

FOSSIL FINDER 91

Quiz Answers 96

Glossary 98

Think of your favourite plant, animal, fungus, or any of the fascinating types of organisms out there. What do you love about it? Is it the earth-covered snout of a badger emerging from her underground home, or the way the morning dew settles on a vibrant buttercup, or the beautiful, but toxic, sheen of a spotty toadstool hidden deep in a forest? Close your eyes and *really* picture it. How did that make you feel? Did you smile?

We need to understand the natural world. We need to admire it. We need to love it to protect it. We probably won't all love all things, but you'll find a lot to smile about if you just look. By making these connections, we can understand the beauty, delicacy and importance of nature. And understanding it gives us a chance of helping our nature-depleted planet and saving many of its wondrous species.

INTRODUCTION

by CHRIS PACKHAM, CBE

Naturalist, broadcaster, author and conservationist.

The fun thing is that it doesn't matter which part of nature you love, because the natural world is all connected. For many of us, dinosaurs are a fascinating part of natural history. I've loved dinosaurs since I was young, and they've helped inspire me to become who I am today.

These brilliant books by Ben are the perfect introduction for every young (or not so young) palaeontologist or budding naturalist. Ben doesn't just provide you with the most up-to-date, fascinating facts, he helps you fall in love with dinosaurs. And let's be honest, who can fail to fall in love with these magnificent, prehistoric predators and huge herbivores?

HEY EVERYONE!

I need you to do a little experiment for me. It's going to sound weird, but remember, weird is good. And anyway, none of us want to be normal. Normal is always less fun than weird. Okay, back to the experiment.

You're going to need a playground. And as many of your classmates as you can find. The experiment happens over three days.

Day 1: go to the playground at lunchtime. Stand in the middle of the playground and close your eyes. Imagine you're a wild animal, a lion or tiger maybe, and give me the biggest roar you can manage. Proper scary, loud enough to shake the glass in the windows and scare the birds from the trees.

Day 2: go back to the playground and do it again. The same as before. But this time, get as many people to join you as you can and roar together.

At this point in the experiment, I need to check something. Was there a difference between the first two days? When I ask that, I want to know if there's any difference in YOUR roar? Of course, there will have been a difference if loads of your classmates joined in on the second day. But what was *your* roar like on the first day? Was it quieter? Did you even roar, or were you a little timid? It's a lot easier to join in with something, so I'm guessing your roar was much better on Day 2. Am I right?

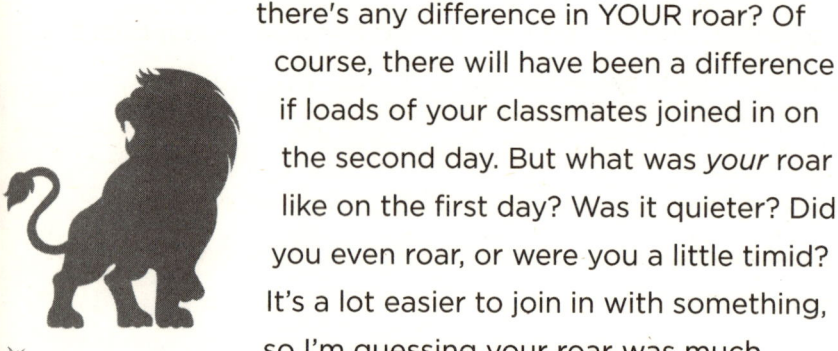

Day 3: it's lunchtime. Go outside on your own. And give me one last roar. Find your inner lion and release your wild voice. Did you notice anything? You may not have been as loud as when you had lots of people around you, but I bet you were louder than you were on Day 1, and I think you'll feel far more confident on Day 3.

Why did I ask you to roar like a lion in your playground over three days? To make you look silly? To see whether your teacher would join in? To find out how loud you can roar? Nope, it's to help you see how we are affected by people around us, and to show you how hard it can be sometimes to do something when you think you're the only one doing it. I used to feel a bit like that when I was your age. I sometimes felt as though I didn't fit in. I loved science and nature but didn't really know anyone else who did. I was a scientist even before I knew I was a scientist, and I loved nature long before I'd even heard it was possible to become a biologist, which is the type of scientist who is lucky enough to study animals, plants and other life forms.

When I was younger, I sometimes felt I was roaring on my own. Then I started meeting other young scientists and people who actually had jobs as scientists. It was like the part of the experiment where you all roared together on Day 2. I felt I had found others who thought like me and liked the same things. It's not always possible to find people who think like you and share the same likes and dislikes, and that's okay too.

Now, as a scientist, I know thousands, maybe even tens of thousands, of other scientists, all around the world. Some work with polar bears in the Arctic and others work with flies in museums. Some are under 10 years old and love plants, and others are nearly 100, and present wildlife programmes on TV.

If you meet people like you, or even just remember there are people like you out there, then your roar will always be louder. I don't mean you'll actually start roaring. Or maybe you will! But really, I mean you'll have a stronger voice and be more confident in the way you think, even when you're on your own again.

Young people like you have come together, all over the world, and have achieved amazing things, either in groups or on their own. Some write books, or campaign to governments or talk on the radio and television. Some clean beaches or plant trees, or raise money, or protect wild species or animals on farms. Some help save habitats and ecosystems. And some help their local community recycle and pick up litter. The thing that ties them and you together, is that combining actions and voices makes the biggest roar. Never believe you can't make a difference, or that you're on your own.

You can change the world, and what's more, we're all here with you.

Ben

CHAPTER 1

DINOSAUR DEFINITIONS

WHAT *IS* A DINOSAUR?

> PLEASED TO MEET YOU.

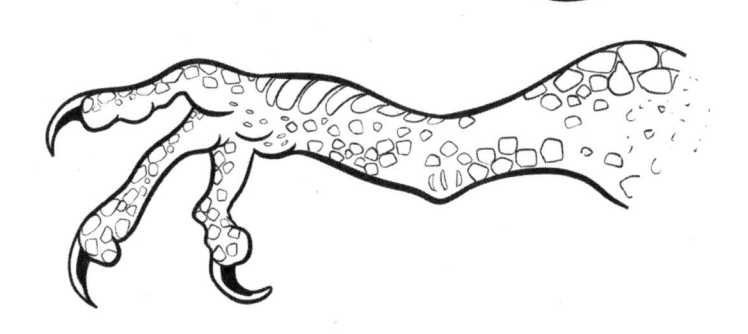

Dinosaur Definitions

What species are you? I'm guessing (and I'm pretty certain about this) that you're human. You're closely related to chimpanzees and gorillas, but if I treated your teeny weeny tiny, microscopic DNA picture like a recipe, it would be unique. No other species of plant or animal would have the same one, no matter how closely related you might be. We can't always look at DNA though, especially if a species is extinct and has been gone for so long that we can no longer read its DNA recipe. When this happens, we have to look for clues on bodies, like some sort of 'spot the difference' puzzle, to see what it is that makes each species special.

This is what we have to do with dinosaurs. They have been extinct for so long, we can no longer look at their DNA. In fact, the oldest DNA scientists have found so far dates from nearly two and a half million years ago from samples discovered in Arctic ice in Greenland, showing species such as lemmings, reindeer, Arctic hares and even horseshoe crabs. Unless we can improve our technology, tests and ways to research, we probably can't look at DNA much older than this. This means we have no chance of looking at the 66-million-year-old DNA from a *Tyrannosaurus rex* in the same way we can for a dodo, mammoth or even a *Neanderthal*.

What *is* a Dinosaur?

Let's get back to deciding whether you're a human or not. I can tell just by looking at you. You walk on two legs, not four. That's a big giveaway. Most of your body isn't covered in a thick coat of hair, and you have quite a flat face. You have hands with five fingers, including a rather special thumb. And you have a chin, which, believe it or not, is something only our species has. There are loads of other things too, but you get my point.

As well as understanding what makes something a dinosaur or not, there is another important question. Why does it matter? Why do we need to know whether something was a dinosaur or not, and, why do we care about dinosaurs at all? Okay, the easy answer is because they're so COOL. It's hard not to like tough armoured beasts battling giant predators with dagger-like teeth, with herbivores taller than trees in the background. You don't have to love them all, but it's difficult to say dinosaurs *aren't* cool. And trust me, everyone has a favourite dinosaur. Go and ask some people now and find out what their favourites are. But why do scientists like dinosaurs and other extinct things? Well, because they can tell us so much, about so many different things.

Dinosaur Definitions

DEFINITELY DINOSAURS

It may seem odd but we don't have an exact definition of what a dinosaur is. This is because there were so many different types. Some were small, some were huge.

Some had two legs, some had four. Some were hunters and others were herbivores. With so many differences, it makes it hard to have a set of rules that works for every fossil. Instead, we use rough guidelines – if a fossil has most of the following, then scientists can be pretty certain they're dealing with a dinosaur.

1. Dinosaurs have two holes behind each eye towards the back of the skull.
This means they are diapsids. If you're wondering, we (as mammals) belong to the synapsid group, all of which have only one hole behind each eye. When you're in your local museum, look at any dinosaur skeleton. The skull should have two holes just behind the eye.

2. Dinosaurs all have straight legs.
Next time you see a crocodile when you're out for a walk, have a look at its legs (just don't get too close).

CROCODILE

Definitely Dinosaurs

Rather than legs that stand straight like ours, their legs bend out in the middle somewhere. All reptiles with legs, such as crocs and their relatives and many lizards, have legs that look the same – they come out from the body to the side and then go down.

DINOSAUR

All dinosaurs (whether with four legs or two) walked with their legs held in a straight line beneath their body. This meant dinosaurs could breathe easily as they walked or ran – great for chasing other dinosaurs, or running away from them. It also allowed them to become much bigger than if they had legs with a bend in the middle.

3. Dinosaurs have short arms. We all know that *Tyrannosaurus rex* and its relatives had teeny arms, but almost every dinosaur had forelimbs slightly

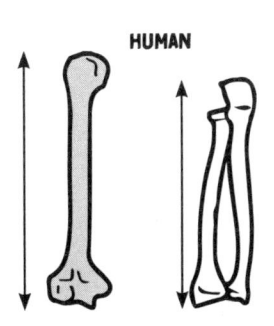

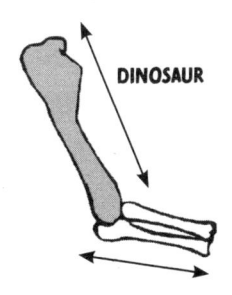

HUMAN

DINOSAUR

Dinosaur Definitions

shorter than you might expect. Have a look at your arms – the upper arm bone (humerus) is only a little longer than the two lower arm bones (radius and ulna). In dinosaurs, the radius is nearly always at least 20 per cent shorter than the humerus.

> So, birds are dinosaurs, hey? How do we know a *Diplodocus*, *Tyrannosaurus rex*, *Oviraptor* and *Thecodontosaurus* are all dinosaurs but that a pterosaur isn't? Are pliosaurs dinosaurs or marine reptiles, and why is a chicken a dinosaur and not a mammal? We need to look at what makes a dinosaur a dinosaur.

There are lots of arguments over dinosaur definitions, because there were so many different species – some small enough to sit on your hand, some big enough to sit on your house (and smash it). Some could glide, some could swim, some could run. Many ate meat, but others ate plants. With so many different dinosaurs, it's hard to make a clear definition.

Definitely Dinosaurs

Try it for yourself with something more familiar like fruit and vegetables – what's the difference? Easy, right? But what about tomatoes? Exactly! Not so easy.

Scientists look at lots of things to see whether they have found a dinosaur fossil. Some seem important and others look as though they couldn't possibly be important – but if we can tick them all off, then we can be 100 per cent sure it's a dinosaur.

DINO CHECKLIST

Some of these things are obvious on some fossils and almost impossible to see on others. To spot them, you will have to *really* know what to look for. Study a dinosaur fossil next time you're at your local museum and then a crocodile or alligator skeleton and maybe a bird. Can you tick these things off in all these skeletons?

If you had x-ray vision and could look at your own skull in the mirror, you would see that you have a hole in your skull behind each eye. This means that we (like all mammals) are **synapsids** (sin-ap sids). But dinosaurs are **diapsids** (di-ap sids). They have two holes behind each eye, towards the back of the skull. **(a)**

Dinosaur Definitions

ANKYLOSAURUS

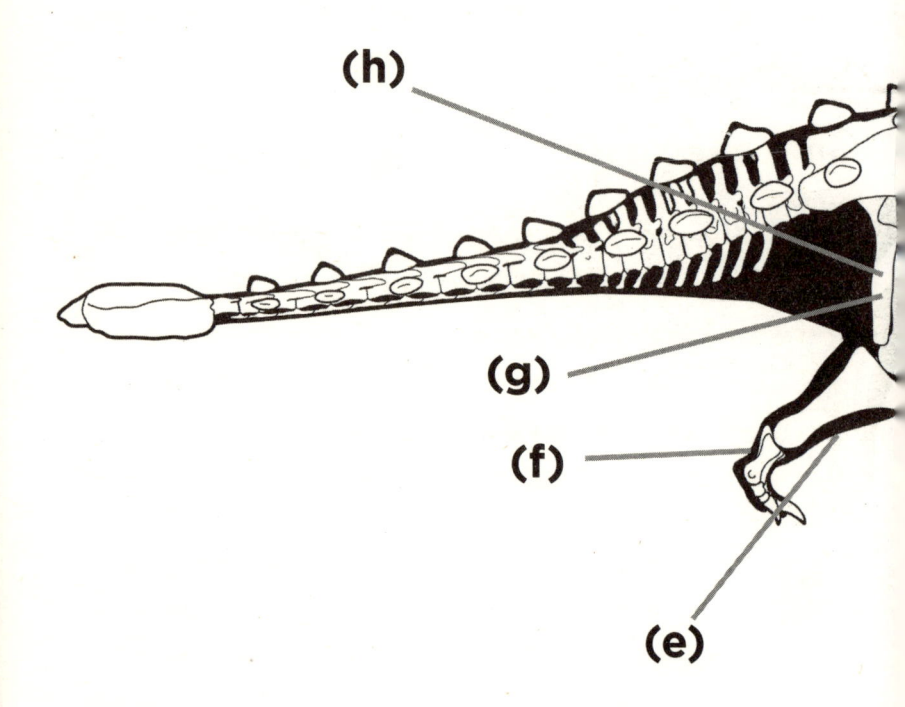

(h)

(g)

(f)

(e)

Dino Checklist

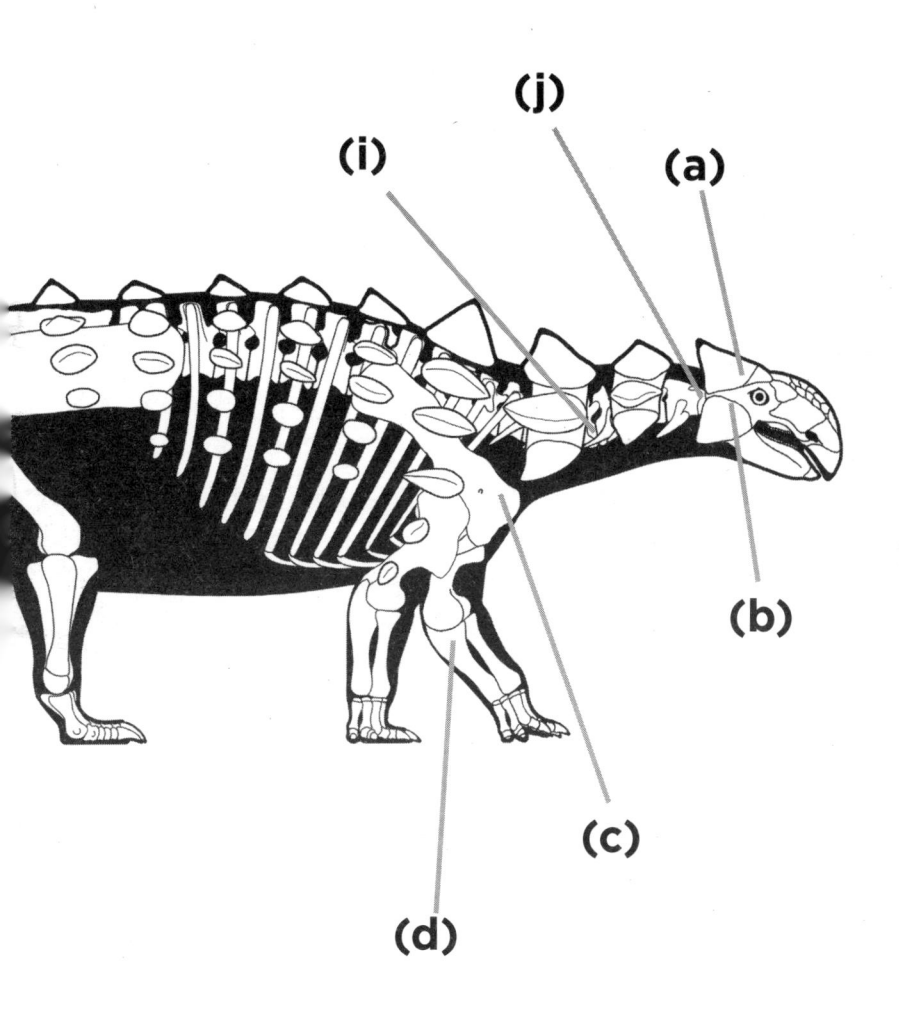

(j)
(i)
(a)
(b)
(c)
(d)

Dinosaur Definitions

Between the two holes behind the eye, there is a dimple (called a **fossa**) in the bone. **(b)**

There is a ridge along the edge of the **humerus** (the upper arm bone) for big muscles to attach to. In dinosaurs, this ridge is more than 30 per cent along the bone. **(c)**

Teeny tiny arms. Almost every dinosaur had **forelimbs** (arms) slightly shorter than you might expect. For most dinosaurs, the **radius** bone (in the lower arm) is nearly always 20 per cent shorter than the **humerus** bone (in the upper arm). **(d)**

The ridge on the **tibia** (shin bone) curves to the front and outwards. **(e)**

At the place where the **fibula** (one of the lower leg bones) joins the ankle, there's a little dip on the ankle bone. **(f)**

Straight legs. Have a look at the people around you – their legs come straight down from their body, not out to the side like a crab. Dinosaurs were the same – their legs were straight, not out to the side. All reptiles (well, those with legs) have legs out to the side. **(g)**

The ridge (called the **fourth trochanter**) on the **femur** (thigh bone), which the big leg muscles attach to, is big and looks sharp. **(h)**

Most of the neck bones (**vertebrae**) have extra bits of bone that look like a diagonally backwards-facing wing on each side. These bits of bones are called '**epipophyses**' (eppi-pofe ee-sees). **(i)**

The bones at the back of the skull do not meet in the middle. **(j)**

CHAPTER 2

DINOSAUR DETECTIVES

Ankylosaurus

Dinosaur Detectives

I often get asked which my favourite dinosaur is, and while I can't tell you my absolute favourite, the amazing *Ankylosaurus* (an-KEE-LO sor-us) has been near the top of my list since I was much younger. This four-legged, spiky dinosaur is famous for its tail, which had a huge bony club at the end, but, as with many dinosaurs, there's much more to learn about *Ankylosaurus*.

First, so we get to know *Ankylosaurus* better, let's do a proper introduction. Like every species, *Ankylosaurus* has a two-part name: *Ankylosaurus magniventris*. *Ankylosaurus* means 'joined-up lizard', because of the way the bones in the skull, and some points on its body, were joined-up, or 'fused', together. *magniventris* (mag-NEE ven-triss) means 'big belly'. There's your introduction to the 'big-bellied, joined-up lizard'.

It's sometimes hard to imagine from films, books and TV programmes how small or big, different dinosaurs were, and sometimes it can be a surprise. Let's start with some of the obvious, more famous, dinosaurs. How long do you think *Diplodocus* was? Well, as one of the longest dinosaurs, it stretched an impressive 32m from its nose to the tip of its tail. That's about as long as

Ankylosaurus

seven cars parked end to end. How much do you think a *Tyrannosaurus rex* weighed? If you think they could weigh as much as two adult African elephants, you'd be about right.

So, what about *Ankylosaurus*? I always thought they were pretty small, maybe the size of a cow... and then I was lucky enough to hold an actual *Ankylosaurus* skull and realised they were much bigger than I'd imagined. The first thing you might be surprised by is that an *Ankylosaurus* weighed between 4 and 8 tonnes, which again is the same as one or two big elephants from Africa, meaning they weighed as much as a *T. rex*. From the tip of its nose to the end of its tail, an adult *Ankylosaurus* would have measured as much as 8m long, which is the same as about eight adult human strides. Although we measure human height from the ground to the tip of your head, we often measure other animals differently, and one way is from the ground to the top of the hip. This way the tallest *Ankylosaurus* measured so far was 1.7m tall at the top of the hip, which is the height of many adult humans.

FAMILY TREE

Although *Ankylosaurus* had quite a few close relatives among the armoured dinosaurs, *Ankylosaurus* was the biggest in the group. In any family, there are always similarities or things that show how the members are related to one another. It's a bit like when people say my little brother and I look similar, even though I don't always think we do.

The bodies of all the armoured dinosaurs, including *Ankylosaurus*, had some things in common, which helps palaeontologists see who was related to who. First, they all had four legs, with big broad bodies. They had fairly long tails and heads that sometimes looked triangular from the top. They didn't all have clubs on their tails, but they did all have bony plates of armour, called osteoderms (oss-TEE-O dermz) covering their body, and bony semi-circular rings around their neck, both for protection.

Family Tree

> Most famously, *Ankylosaurus* had a fascinating tail, with a huge bony club at the tip. It also had spikes and spines across different parts of its body, which would also have helped protect it from predators and in fights with other armoured dinosaurs.

Not long ago, a friend of mine looked into my family tree for me, and we found all sorts of people I'd never heard of but was still related to. I was fascinated by what their jobs were, where they lived, and in some cases, how they died. But the research only went back a little over 200 years, and even then, we don't have complete information.

Dinosaur Detectives

FAMILY TREE

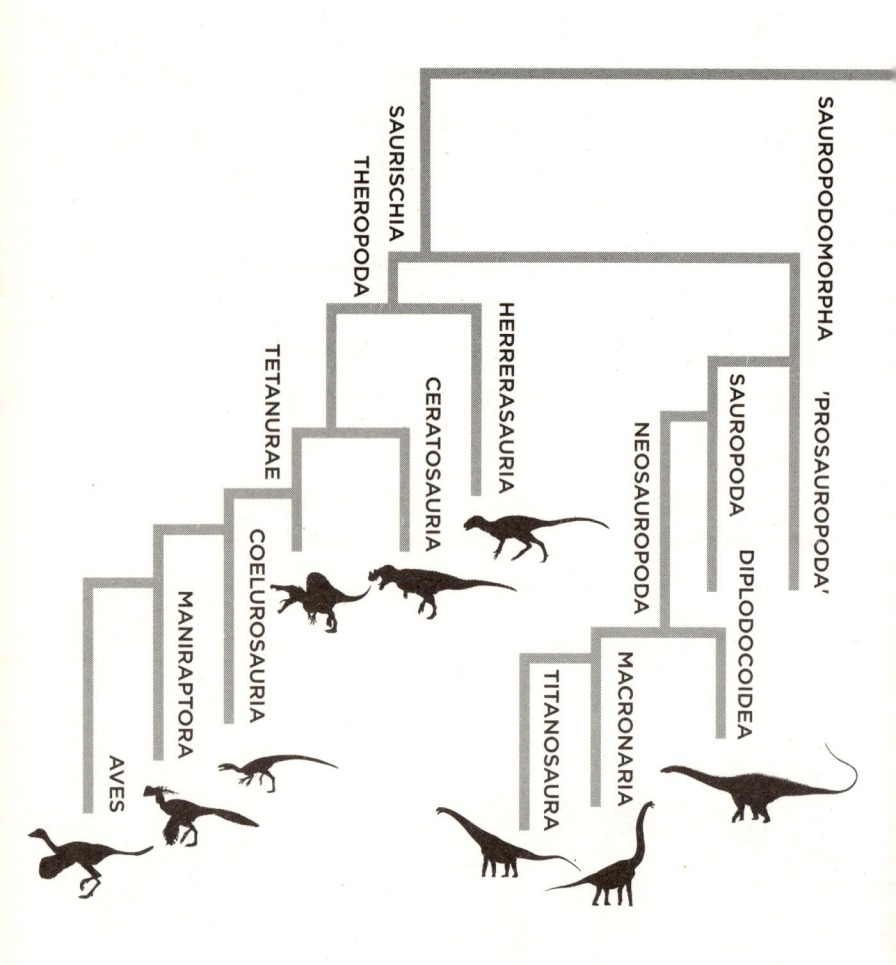

Family Tree

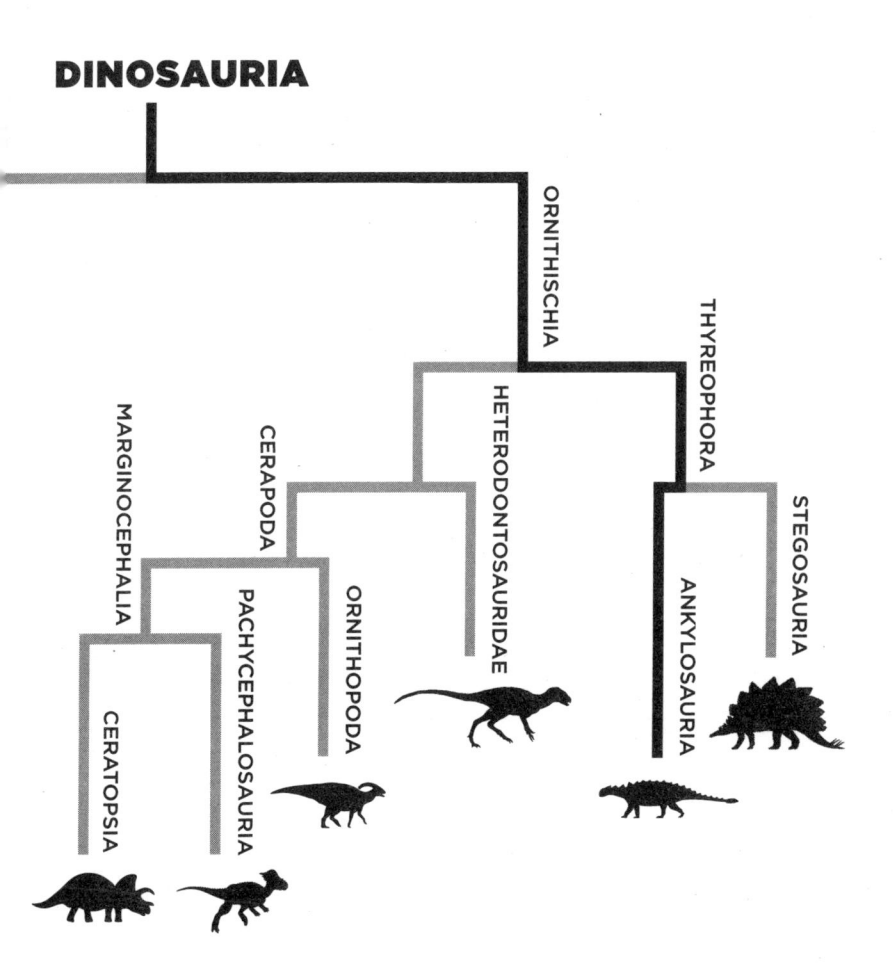

DINOSAURIA

- ORNITHISCHIA
  - HETERODONTOSAURIDAE
  - CERAPODA
    - ORNITHOPODA
    - MARGINOCEPHALIA
      - PACHYCEPHALOSAURIA
      - CERATOPSIA
  - THYREOPHORA
    - ANKYLOSAURIA
    - STEGOSAURIA

ORNITHISCHIA

Thyreophora

Imagine trying to put a family tree together for a dinosaur, which lived millions and millions of years ago. This is what we are trying to do with *Ankylosaurus*. A really cool family tree, but one which still has lots of gaps.

We know that *Ankylosaurus* belonged to a very big group of dinosaurs, called the Ornithischia (or-nith iss-KEE-a), which are also known as the 'bird-hipped' dinosaurs. This big group includes the stegosaurs, the hadrosaurs, and the horned dinosaurs, including the famous *Triceratops*, as well as *Ankylosaurus* and its armoured relatives.

Within that big group are smaller groups. One of these is called Thyreophora (THI-REE-O phor-a) which means 'shield bearers' and is often just called the 'armoured dinosaurs'. Within *this* group, we see two smaller groups. First, Ankylosauria (an-KEE-LO sor-EE-a), which contains *Ankylosaurus* and its closest relatives, and Stegosauria (steg-O sor-EE-a), which

Family Tree

Ankylosauria — Nodosauridae
Ankylosauridae
Ankylosaurus

Stegosauria
Stegosaurus

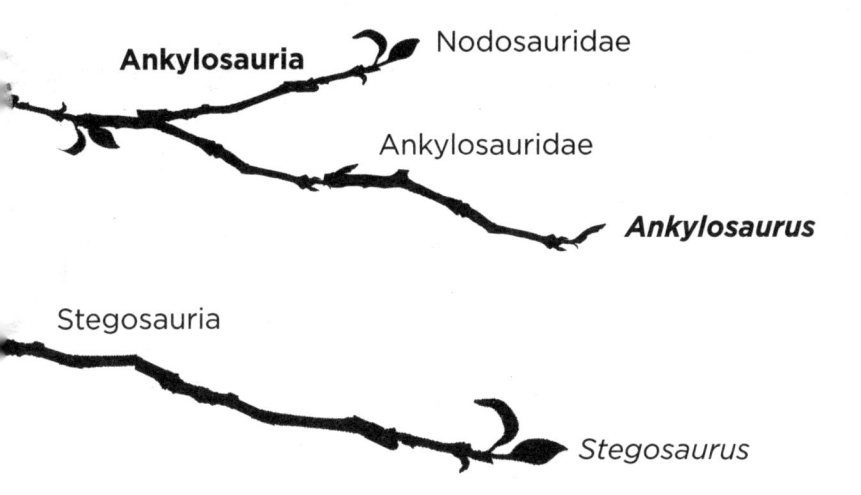

contains *Stegosaurus* and its closest relatives, meaning *Ankylosaurus* was closely related to *Stegosaurus*, another very cool spiky, armoured herbivore.

Within the Ankylosauria group, there are two more splits. One is Nodosauridae (no-doh -sor-id-AY) or the nodosaurs, and the other is Ankylosauridae (an-KEE-LO sor-id-AY), or the ankylosaurs. You've done well if you've understood this far, because these are the sort of technical family relationships scientists spend years studying. It looks as though our understanding of the *Ankylosaurus* family tree will change though, as we find more fossil evidence and more pieces of the puzzle.

Dinosaur Detectives

TEST YOUR DINO KNOWLEDGE HERE!

How much did *Ankylosaurus* weigh?

Name other dinosaurs who belong to the 'bird-hipped' group of Ornithischia.

What covered all armoured dinosaurs' bodies?

What did *Ankylosaurus* measure from the tip of its nose to the tip of its tail?

All the answers are in the text and at the back of the book.

ANKYLOSAURUS **RELATIVES**

Zuul (ZOOL) Named after a scary-looking monster in the film *Ghostbusters*.

The full name for this dinosaur is *Zuul crurivastator* (ZOOL CRU-REE vass-TAY-tor) and it was a member of the ankylosaur group of armoured dinosaurs. The name *Zuul* comes from the film *Ghostbusters*, which had a ferocious-looking monster in it. The story goes that when this dinosaur was discovered, it reminded the team of the demon from the film. *Crurivastator* comes from two Latin words which means 'destroyer of shins'. Not far from where *Zuul* was discovered, the fossil skeleton from a relative of *T. rex*, called *Gorgosaurus*, was found with a badly broken shin bone, which had luckily healed. Although we'll never know for sure what happened to this unlucky predator, one possible theory is that it was whacked by the tail of an unhappy *Zuul*, which lived in the same place, at the same time, around 75 million years ago.

Dinosaur Detectives

Gastonia (gass-tone-EE-a) Named after a palaeontologist, called Robert Gaston.

While *Ankylosaurus* was famous for its tail club, not all of its close relatives had the same tail, and in fact, many members of the group had a longer tail, without a club. *Gastonia* was an early member of the group and lived between 139 million to 125 million years ago, in what is now North America. It was one of the armoured dinosaurs that did not have a tail club. It had a large bony shield which rested over its hips and bum and large spikes which sat up on its shoulders. It was smaller than its larger relative, measuring just 5m long, and weighing just under 2 tonnes. It's still not fully agreed whether *Gastonia* was closely related to *Ankylosaurus*, or whether it sat in the slightly more distantly related group called the nodosaurs.

Gargoyleosaurus (gar-goyl EE-o sor-us) 'gargoyle lizard'

Gargoyleosaurus was among the earliest ankylosaurs from the nodosaur group. It lived during the late Jurassic, between 154 million and 150 million years ago, in what is now North America. Measuring just over 3m long and weighing between 300–750kg, (about as much as a dairy cow), *Gargoyleosaurus* was much smaller than *Ankylosaurus*.

It may not sound much, but a key feature of this little dinosaur is that it had a bony armoured plate in the middle of one of the rows of armour – most other members of the group had pairs of bony plates. This shows that sometimes even small features are important to palaeontologists when identifying new and different animals. Like many of its relatives, *Gargoyleosaurus* also lacked a big tail club.

Dinosaur Detectives

Edmontonia (ed-mon tone-EE-a) Named after the Edmonton rock layers where the fossils were found.

With two closely related species of *Edmontonia*, this was a fairly large type of nodosaur dinosaur, weighing around 3 tonnes and measuring about 6.5m long. The skull of *Edmontonia* measured up to 50cm and was quite long, especially around the snout or nose area. At the end of this snout *Edmontonia* had a horny beak, with no teeth at the front of the mouth. Behind the beak, in the upper jaw, it had 14–17 teeth on each side. On the lower jaw, the number of teeth was between 18–21 on each side, meaning *Edmontonia* had between 64–76 small teeth.

CHAPTER 3

DINOSAUR DISCOVERIES

WHEN AND WHERE

Dinosaur Discoveries

WHEN AND WHERE

The times when dinosaurs existed can be split into three main chunks (what we call 'periods') and these are the **Triassic period**, the **Jurassic period** and the **Cretaceous period**. *Ankylosaurus* was around at the end of the Cretaceous period. It lived between 68-66 million years ago. Fossils have been found across western North America, in states such as Montana and Wyoming, and in Canada, in Alberta and Saskatchewan.

During the Cretaceous, there were more types of dinosaur than at any other time and there were lots of different types of armoured dinosaurs in addition to *Ankylosaurus*. The ankylosaur group of dinosaurs was only found in the northern hemisphere, which is the part of the world above the equator. Their fossils have been discovered in western North America, Europe and East Asia, and the oldest of these fossils dates to around 100 million years ago.

It might surprise you, but the world hasn't always looked as it does today. For millions and millions of years, most of the land was lumped together in a single big chunk, which was called a 'supercontinent'. Towards the end

When and Where

of the Cretaceous period, this supercontinent started to break up and very slowly different parts drifted away, starting the journey of the smaller continents we see around us today. *Ankylosaurus* lived throughout what is now North America, but what was known as Laramidia (la-ra mid-E-ah) at the end of the Cretaceous.

THE WORLD IN THE LATE CRETACEOUS PERIOD

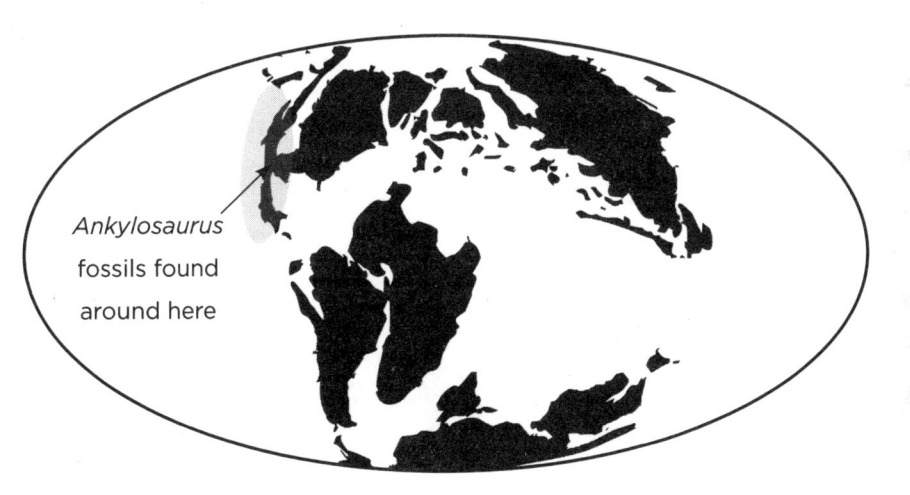

Ankylosaurus fossils found around here

Laramidia was an island continent, and it stretched from what is now Alaska in the north, to Mexico in the south. This is a rich area for fossils, and everything from *Tyrannosaurus rex* and *Triceratops*, to troodons (TROO o-dons) and pachycephalosaurs (pak-EE-seff a-lo-sors) have been found throughout this area.

Dinosaur Discoveries

***Ankylosaurus* fossils are found in this period only**

CRETACEOUS PERIOD

Mesozoic era

JURASSIC PERIOD

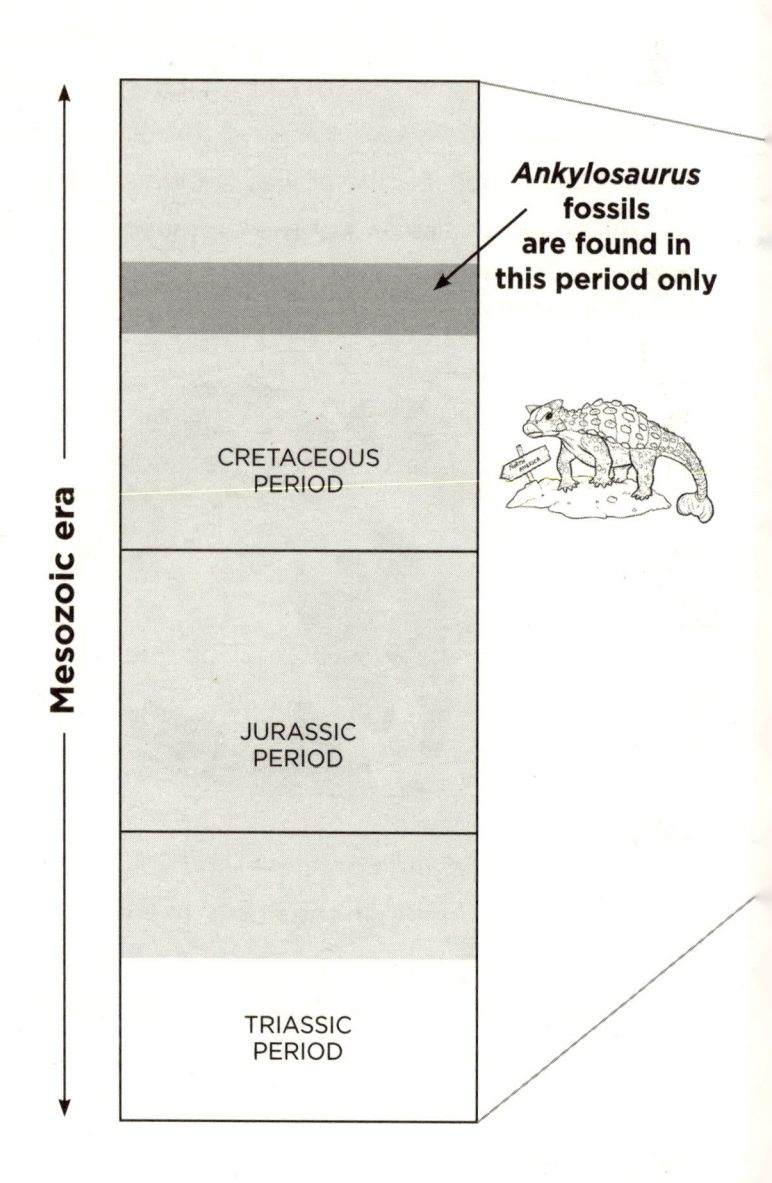

TRIASSIC PERIOD

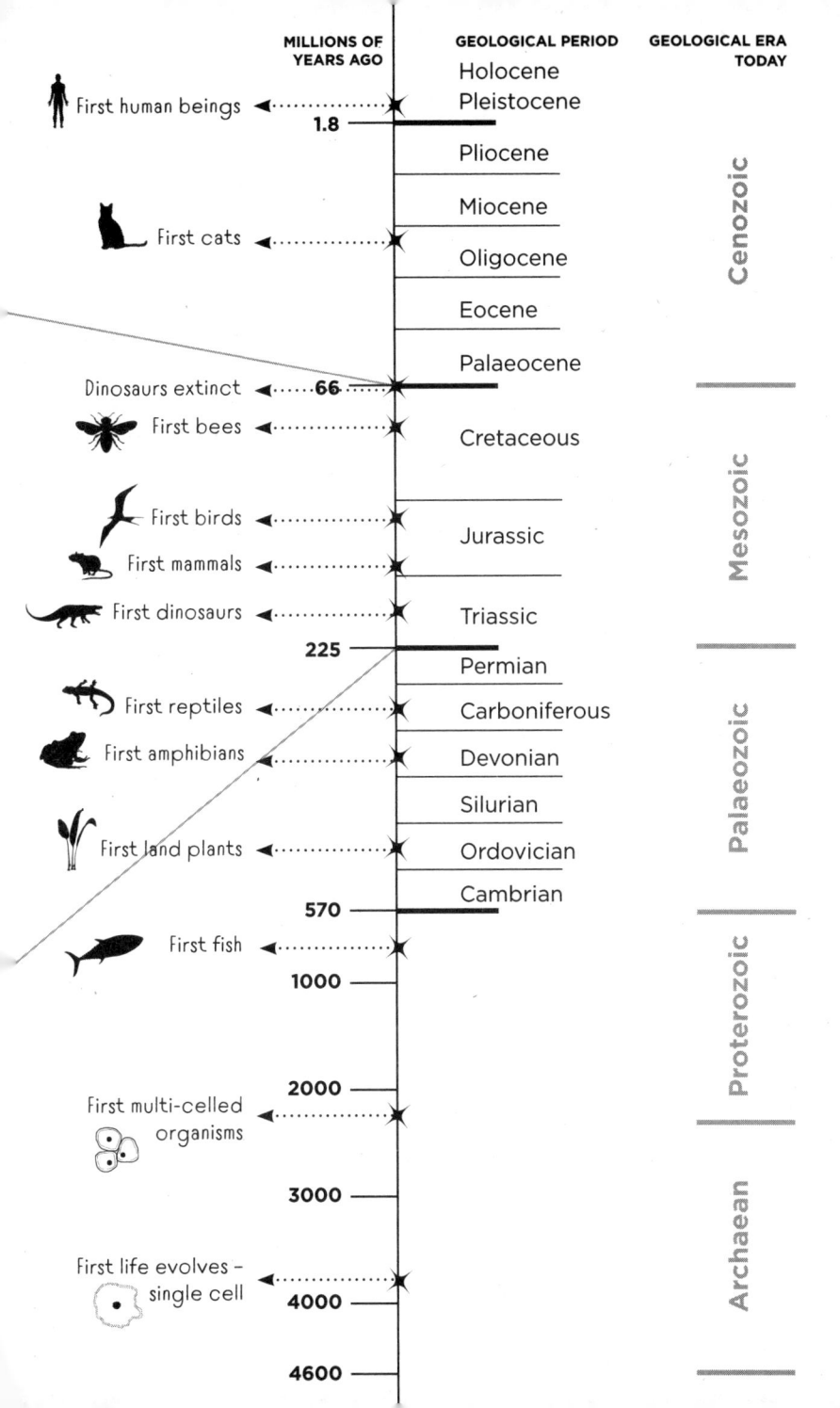

	MILLIONS OF YEARS AGO	GEOLOGICAL PERIOD	GEOLOGICAL ERA TODAY
First human beings	1.8	Holocene / Pleistocene	Cenozoic
		Pliocene	
First cats		Miocene	
		Oligocene	
		Eocene	
		Palaeocene	
Dinosaurs extinct	66		
First bees		Cretaceous	Mesozoic
First birds		Jurassic	
First mammals			
First dinosaurs		Triassic	
	225	Permian	
First reptiles		Carboniferous	Palaeozoic
First amphibians		Devonian	
		Silurian	
First land plants		Ordovician	
	570	Cambrian	
First fish			
	1000		Proterozoic
	2000		
First multi-celled organisms			
	3000		Archaean
First life evolves – single cell	4000		
	4600		

TYRANNOSAURUS REX

ANKYLOSAURUS

TRICERATOPS

TROODON

PACHYCEPHALOSAURUS

WOULD DINOSAURS MAKE GOOD PETS?

ASK AN EXPERT

**So many people work with dinosaurs –
from amateur collectors to world-famous scientists.
Some go looking for fossils in the ground, others study
them in laboratories and some recreate them
as incredible pieces of artwork.**

DR JESS FRENCH

Vet, author and TV presenter

Dr French has worked with animals all over the world.
She writes books about the natural world, its amazing
inhabitants and what we can do to save them.

We asked Jess the following question:

'Would dinosaurs make good pets?'

And this is what she told us:

That's a *really easy* question, because I have five pet dinosaurs of my own and they make BRILLIANT pets. They live in my back garden, where they scrabble around in the dirt, gobbling up worms and digging up my favourite plants. My dinosaurs are pretty easy to look after, they love a cuddle, and most days they give me a delicious egg for my breakfast. I would highly recommend keeping them.

Not the answer you expected? Well, of course, I'm talking about my pet chickens. I'm hoping some of you will know that scientists lumped birds and dinosaurs together in the big classification system we use to understand how different animals are related to one another. Scientists realised birds and dinosaurs were so similar, birds should be classed as living dinosaurs. And while chicken-keeping is a form of dinosaur-keeping, it doesn't fully answer the question. It's a bit like the following conversation:

You: Is all fruit red and juicy?

Me: Yes. Strawberries are bright red and deliciously juicy.

You: But what about bananas? And melons?

My answer about dinosaurs doesn't quite cover the whole story, does it? And, as you know, from reading Prof Ben's brilliant books, there are many and varied dinosaurs each as different as strawberries and melons. Perhaps even *more* different. There are big dinosaurs and small ones, stompy dinosaurs and snappy ones. We know of small predators that could have easily fitted into your pocket, and huge herbivores larger than a house and heavier than a whale. Some dinosaurs were armoured, some could fly and others could swim. They came in lots of different sizes and shapes.

So how do we work out which dinosaurs would have made good pets? In order to care for a pet properly, we need to be able to provide it with:

1. Suitable food
2. Freedom to act normally
3. A comfortable place to live
4. Freedom from fear
5. Access to veterinary care

So, let's see how this works with our favourite *T. rex*

1. Do you have any dead dinosaurs hanging around or ideally a field full of smaller herbivores (let's call them prey for now) to feed to it? ✗

2. Are you looking for an animal companion that would happily eat you too? ✗

3. Its hutch would need to be the size of your house. And this is just the bare minimum space you'd need. For a happy *T. rex*, you'd most likely need a couple of hundred kilometres for its territory. ✗

4. It wouldn't be scared of you, your dog or anything else, except perhaps a bigger, hungrier *T. rex*. ✓

5. Good luck finding a vet willing to treat a *T. rex*. ✗

What about *Compsognathus*?

1. You'd need to buy it small animals to eat, such as frozen mice and chicks, or if it's loose in the garden maybe even the squirrels and some of the birds at your bird feeder. ✓

2. It loved to run, so be prepared for some off-lead walking. ✓

3. It was about the size of a turkey, you'd need a shed or outbuilding to house it. ✓

4. I presume there are no *Archeopteryx* flying around your garden? ✓

5. Any vet willing to treat an ostrich or turkey would probably make an exception for a *Compsognathus*. ✓

Well there you have it!

Different dinosaurs would have required different levels of care and veterinary support. Many of us do keep dinosaurs today, such as chickens, ducks, budgies and parrots, but in my professional opinion, I don't think it would have been a great idea to keep any of the extinct dinosaurs as pets, regardless of how small they were.

CHAPTER 4

DELVE INTO A DINOSAUR

ANATOMY OF *ANKYLOSAURUS*

Delve into a Dinosaur

THE BONES

Of all the dinosaurs we know so far, *Ankylosaurus* is one of THE most unusual looking, but one of the easiest to recognise. We know it was a big dinosaur, which walked on four legs. It had lots of spikes and armour and that amazing tail with a huge club at the end which could be used to smash into predators, such as *Tyrannosaurus rex*. It's obvious, right? Well, what if you knew that we have never found a complete *Ankylosaurus* skeleton, and that we only have pieces from skeletons?

Imagine trying to know all there is to know about a particular species when you only have a few skulls and bits and pieces from skeletons. How certain would you be that your ideas were right? How sure would you be that you'd placed the spikes in the right places? Could your idea about the size of the animal be wrong? Find a photo of a hippopotamus skull and ask a friend, teacher or family member to guess what sort of animal has a skull like that – it's easy to think it might come from some sort of mix of monster and alien.

THE SKULL

Sometimes, it's hard to look at something in nature and see what it's for. It's taken several hundred years to figure out that the long tusk of a narwhal isn't for spearing fish but is actually used for a range of things, including possibly testing the level of salt in water and even acting as a thermometer.

But sometimes, it's much easier to see exactly what's going on, and the *Ankylosaurus* skull is a great example of that. It's as if someone has designed a heavy duty safe that needs to protect what's inside at all costs, and it also needs to be able to see, smell, hear and eat. The *Ankylosaurus* had one of the most heavily armoured and best-protected skulls ever seen in nature.

Delve into a Dinosaur

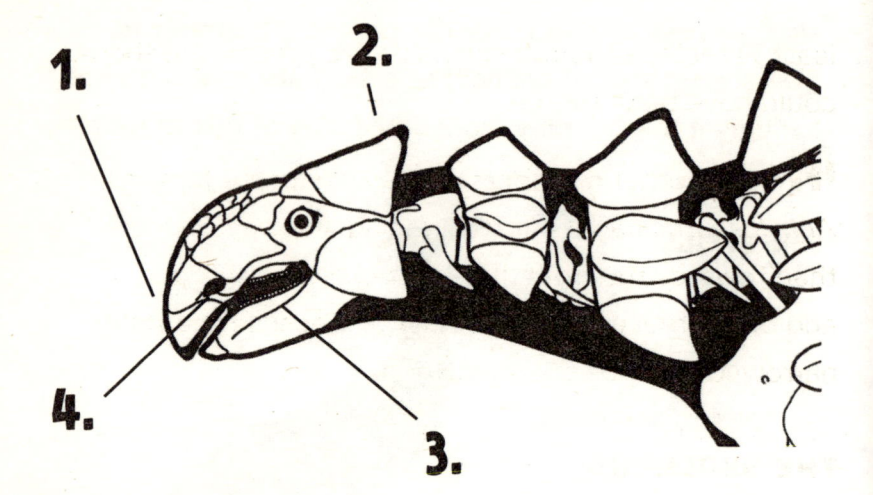

1. Only three skulls have been found and each looks quite different. The largest fossil skull found so far measured 64.5cm long and 74.5cm wide. It was triangular in shape, with a beak at the front of its mouth and lots of small, leaf-shaped teeth.

2. Two horns, which pointed backwards, were at the back of the skull, and two horns below these pointed back and down. These were most likely for *Ankylosaurus* to defend itself against predators, or for display to others of its own species, or a combination of both.

3. Not all parts of the skull have been found yet, but from what we do have, we know *Ankylosaurus* had at least 71 teeth, although scientists are pretty sure there could have been more.

4. Unlike other members of the ankylosaur family, *Ankylosaurus* had its nostrils facing sideways rather than towards the front. Its eye sockets were round and did not face directly sideways, because the skull narrowed towards the snout.

THE SKELETON

1. The weight, and centre of gravity, was low to the ground.

2. Bony armour plating covered most of the top of the body, for protection.

3. To make the tail 'handle', the last seven bones in the tail were all joined together.

4. Semi-circular tail club was made up from two large chunks of bone, called osteoderms.

5. The back legs were longer than the front legs.

6. Scientists think each back foot had three toes.

Delve into a Dinosaur

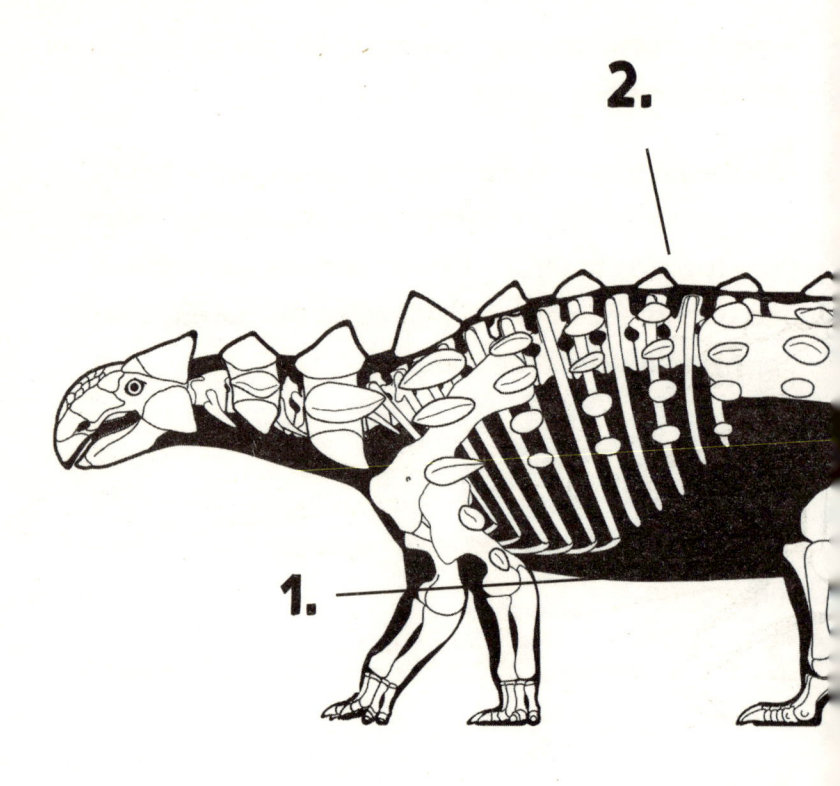

2.

1.

Sometimes, the best weapon is defence. This is certainly the case for *Ankylosaurus*. They weren't fast and it doesn't appear as though they lived in big social groups, like some other dinosaurs did. This means that *Ankylosaurus* could have been seen as a very big breakfast, lunch or dinner for any large predatory

The Skeleton

3.

4.

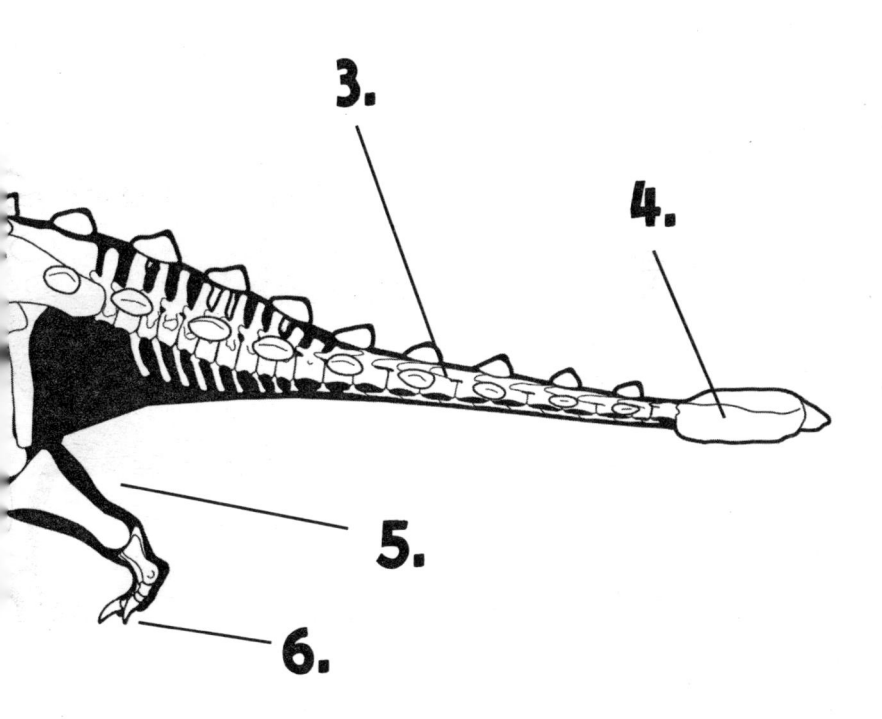

5.

6.

dinosaur around at the time, such as the one and only *T. rex*. As we'll see though, the body of this dinosaur had so many special adaptations, it would have been almost impossible for a predator to successfully attack and kill an adult *Ankylosaurus*.

Delve into a Dinosaur

THE BODY

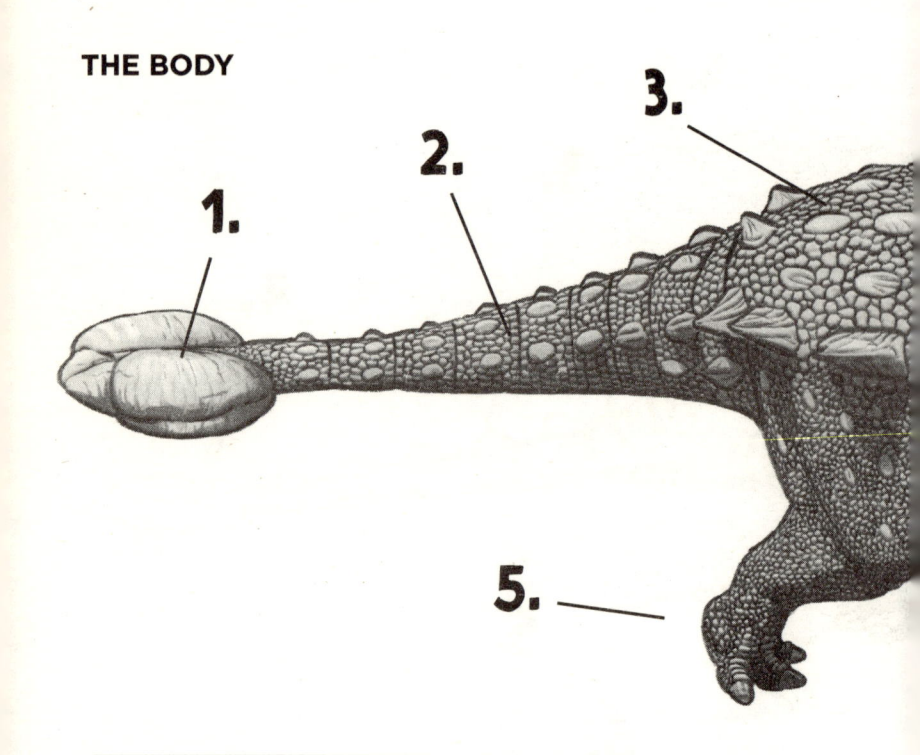

1.

2.

3.

5.

With each new discovery, our understanding of *Ankylosaurus* grows. For a long time, it was thought *Ankylosaurus* was fat and quite short from nose to tail. But from the most recent findings, scientists think it may have been a lot longer and quite a bit thinner. *Ankylosaurus* has had a bit of a palaeontological make-over.

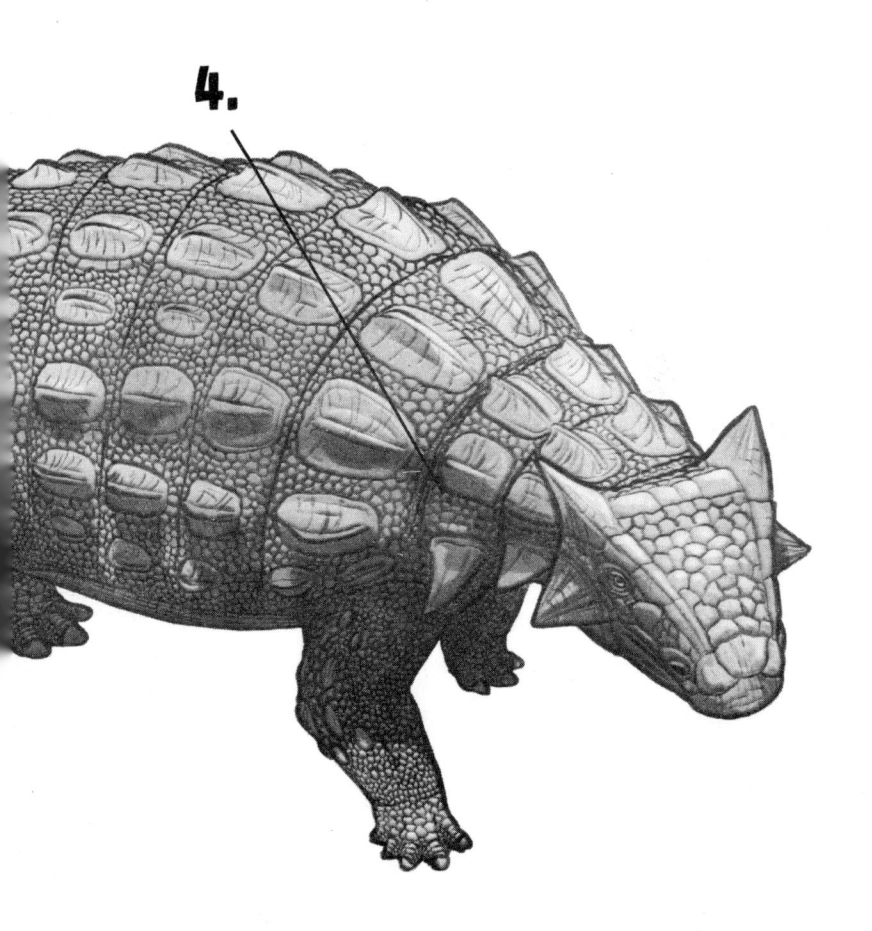

The Body

4.

Delve into a Dinosaur

1. The famous *Ankylosaurus* tail was made up from two parts, the 'knob' at the end, and the 'handle', which is the long bit of the tail. The knob was made up from two large bones, called osteoderms (os-TEE-O dermz), which are usually found inside the skin of some animals. These tail osteoderms were huge and would have been used for display or defence, or maybe both. There would also have been two smaller osteoderms at the tip of the tail, and a line of them running along the middle of the tail, along the top.

You might not believe this, but we only have one tail club from one *Ankylosaurus*, which means we need to find more before we know more about them. The one we do have measures 60cm long, 49cm wide, and 19cm tall. Try drawing this, or make your own tail club out of sand next time you're on the beach, to get an idea of how big it was. The longest *Ankylosaurus* tail measured so far is 216cm ... which is a lot more than a tall human being. When scientists tried measuring how far the tail could swing from side to side, they predicted it could have swung 100 degrees. When you are trying to imagine how far this is, the edges of a sheet of paper make a 90 degree angle, so it's a bit wider than that.

A big question is how powerful was a swinging *Ankylosaurus* tail knob? Could it smash the bones of predators, and if so, how much damage could it cause? In the same way we measure length in centimetres (cm) or kilometres (km), or temperature in degrees Celsius (°C), we can measure the power of something by looking at its force. The unit we use to measure this is called the Newton (N).

When we look at the force created by a swinging *Ankylosaurus* tail, scientists found it was able to hit something with a force of as much as 1,100 N. When we try and predict how much force this meant in a very small area, this works out to be the same as 5,600 N in an area measuring 1cm by 1cm. More than enough to smash the strongest bone. It's about the same force as a hyena biting with its bone-crushing jaws. When we look at other dinosaurs, we see this was more than twice the force of a *Stegosaurus* tail spike, which could create a strike of 510 N, or 1,800 N if we think about the same force in that same little square centimetre area.

Delve into a Dinosaur

2. To make sure the powerful tail knob didn't cause injuries to the *Ankylosaurus* itself, the rest of the tail needed to be quite stiff, and well supported. There's a lot more information on this and why it's important in the 'New Science' section. The last seven tail bones, or vertebrae (ver-ter BRAY) were joined together. When we see bones permanently stuck together like this, we say they are 'fused'. Usually, the space between two bones has a slippery material called cartilage (car-til adge). This is the same stuff as in your ears and nose, but when it's between bones, it allows them to move against each other without causing injury. The weird thing is that in the last seven bones in the tail of *Ankylosaurus*, there is no cartilage between these bones. If they moved, this would cause a lot of pain and a lot of damage. Instead, we see they could not move and were even reinforced with special bony strips holding them in place. This part of the tail is called the 'handle'.

The Body

3. Apart from the tail, the other thing *Ankylosaurus* is notable for is that it was absolutely covered in spines and plates of armour. It was possibly the ultimate armoured dinosaur. Its armour was made up from specialised, flattened pieces of bones called scutes or osteoderms which form inside the skin. These are the same sort of bones found in the tail 'knob'. They're also the same sort of flattened bony armour in crocodiles and their relatives, and armadillos. These osteoderms formed rows found down the animal's neck, back and hips. There were smaller ones across its body and between the larger osteoderms. Some of the smallest osteoderms were 1cm across, whereas the biggest were over 35.5cm wide.

4. Although *Ankylosaurus* is a well-known and popular dinosaur, there is still a lot we don't know about it, including much about its skeleton and body. We especially want to know more about its pelvis, its feet and that distinctive tail. We know, for example, that in one big adult, the humerus (HEW-mer us) which is the bone between your elbow and shoulder, measured about 54cm long and was broad, making it very strong. The femur (FEE-mer), which is the bone sitting between your knee and hip, was 67cm long and was also strong, to support such a very large animal.

5. Although we don't know for sure yet, scientists think *Ankylosaurus* had three toes on each of its back legs. The fossils haven't been found, so we're basing this on fossils from similar species, where the fossils have shown three toes.

This is a tough experiment but stand up and lean forward while keeping your legs and the rest of your body as straight as possible. Here's the tricky part – you have to really take notice of your body, because you're trying to see how close you can get to tipping over, without actually tipping over. And at *that* point, that 'nearly tipping over' point, you're trying to feel where it is in your body that feels like it's pulling you too far forward. Is it your head? Your chest? Your legs? Well, I can tell you now if your body is in a straight line, you should feel that tipping point down in your belly. It's the point where your body has its balance. We call this our centre of gravity. For humans, it's low down in our body, because we walk on two legs. Our nearest relatives in nature, chimpanzees, walk on four legs, and their centre of gravity is much higher up, in their chest.

Ankylosaurus had a very low centre of gravity, which would definitely have been helpful. By having a point of balance so close to the ground the animal wasn't top heavy, which meant it would have been difficult to topple over. This would have made it extra safe from predators, who would not have been able to tip the armoured dinosaur over to get to the softer, squishier parts underneath.

This did come with a possible problem though. Compared to an *Ankylosaurus*, elephants have a high centre of gravity. This allows them to push against trees and knock them over to get at the tasty leaves. Because *Ankylosaurus* had a low centre of gravity, it probably couldn't knock trees down to get at the leaves, so it couldn't get food in the same way. While elephants are responsible for changing their environments by knocking down trees, it is unlikely *Ankylosaurus* was able to change its own surroundings in the same way.

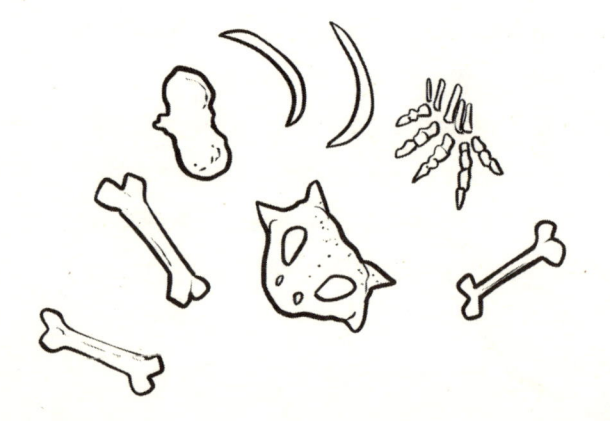

CHAPTER 5

DINOSAUR DOMAINS

HABITATS AND ECOSYSTEMS

Dinosaur Domains

HABITATS AND ECOSYSTEMS

The dinosaurs were around for about 170 million years – that's an incredible amount of time. So, imagine the chances of two different dinosaur species being alive at the same time. Pretty small, right? When *Ankylosaurus* was alive, between 68–66 million years ago, at the end of the Cretaceous period, *loads* of the best known dinosaurs were around at the same time. Fossils from North America show us that while *Ankylosaurus* was munching on plants, some of the most recognisable dinosaurs ever, including *Triceratops* and the mighty *Tyrannosaurus rex,* were in the same environment. How many do you recognise?

If we want to know what *Ankylosaurus* was like, we need to understand what its home was like. What sort of environment did *Ankylosaurus* live in? Palaeontologists have been able to show that *Ankylosaurus*, along with *Triceratops*, *Edmontosaurus* (ed-mont-O sor-us) and *Tyrannosaurus rex* lived along western parts of what is now North America. During the Late Cretaceous, this area would have been a

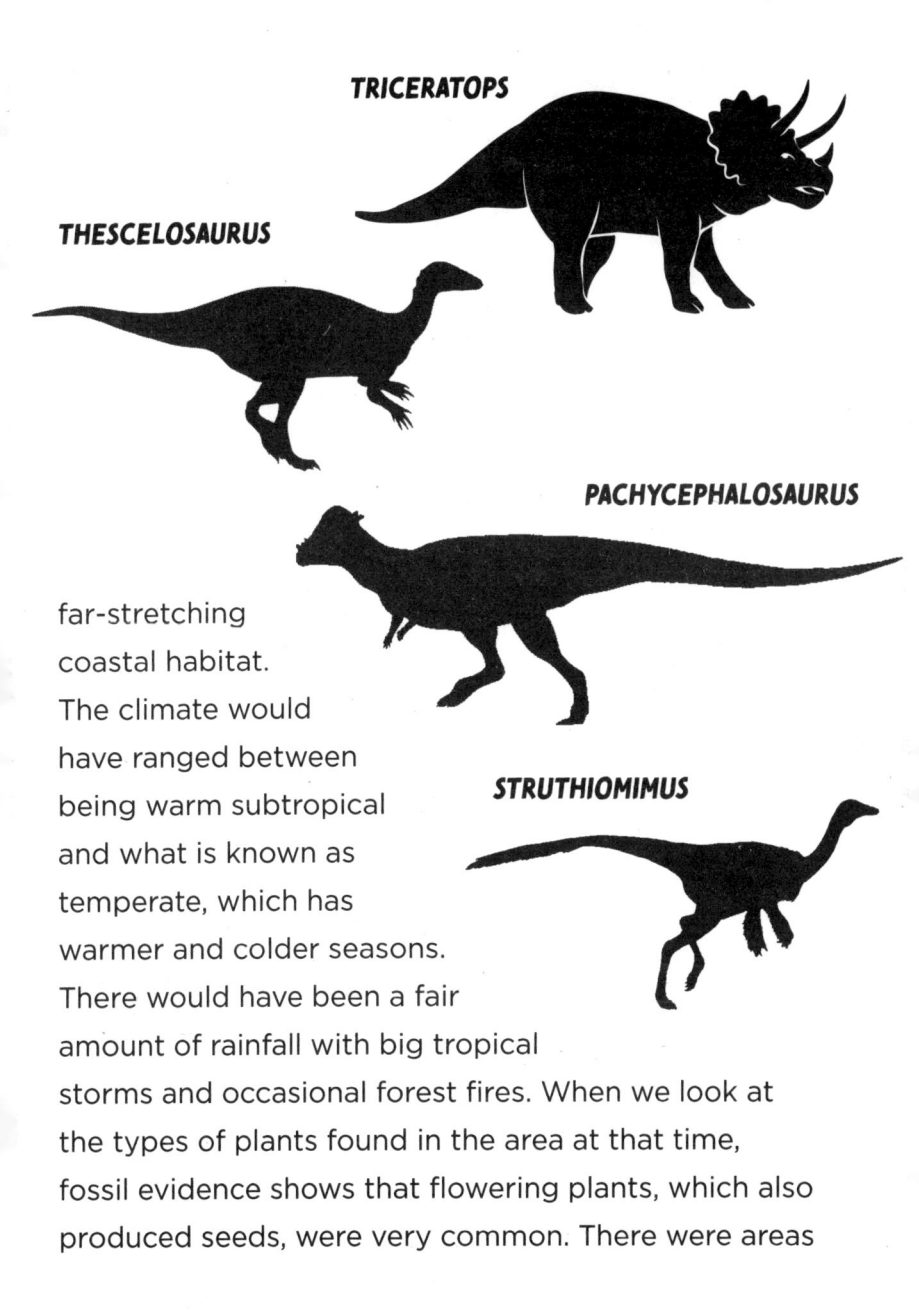

Habitats and Ecosystems

TRICERATOPS

THESCELOSAURUS

PACHYCEPHALOSAURUS

STRUTHIOMIMUS

far-stretching coastal habitat. The climate would have ranged between being warm subtropical and what is known as temperate, which has warmer and colder seasons. There would have been a fair amount of rainfall with big tropical storms and occasional forest fires. When we look at the types of plants found in the area at that time, fossil evidence shows that flowering plants, which also produced seeds, were very common. There were areas

Dinosaur Domains

EDMONTOSAURUS

of thick forest, which were full of small trees. There would also have been evergreen conifers and ferns in the environment, too. It's possible to piece together what sort of plants *Ankylosaurus* would have eaten, by looking at different parts of its body, such as its teeth, and the types of plant fossils found in the area. Because *Ankylosaurus* had small, leaf-shaped teeth, rather than big chunky teeth, it's most likely it ate leaves close to the ground, stripping them from plant stems.

In nature, it's rare to have two similar types of animals which eat exactly the same thing in the same place at the same time. It causes competition between them. We see something similar with *Ankylosaurus* fossils. Another armoured dinosaur, *Edmontonia* (ed-mon toe-NEE-a) was found in the same area, but not at exactly the same time as *Ankylosaurus*. They evolved to live in different areas. *Ankylosaurus* fossils have been found

PECTINODON

Habitats and Ecosystems

in hilly locations whereas *Edmontonia* fossils have been found mostly in areas that were low, close to sea level. That means even if they were around at the same time, they probably wouldn't have met each other.

> A question we still have about *Ankylosaurus* is why we haven't found many fossils yet. This might be because, when they were alive, they were very rare animals. Fewer animals means fewer fossils. Another idea is that fossils form better in muddy, watery areas, meaning animals living in drier, higher areas, such as the *Ankylosaurus*, were less likely to be turned into fossils. Right now, we don't know why there aren't many fossils for this fantastic species.

TYRANNOSAURUS REX

Dinosaur Domains

TEST YOUR DINO KNOWLEDGE HERE!

What was the name of the supercontinent that started to break up towards the end of the Cretaceous?

How many teeth do scientists believe *Ankylosaurus* had?

How long is the longest *Ankylosaurus* tail measured so far?

Why did a low centre of gravity help *Ankylosaurus*?

What did *Ankylosaurus* eat?

All the answers are in the text and at the back of the book.

HOW ANKYLOSAURUS GOT ITS TAIL

NEW SCIENCE

WHERE DID THAT COME FROM?

Imagine a house. Try to picture it in your mind and see the different parts. Now imagine you have to build your own house . . . where would you start? I hope you're not thinking of building the roof first, because it wouldn't be able to float in the air on its own, would it? I don't think you'll be picking the colour for the paint on the walls, or the patterns for the carpets and curtains if you haven't made sure there are floors and windows in place first. It might sound obvious, and even a little silly, but when we're looking at complicated things, we need to do so in a certain order, to make sure we're doing it properly. We follow a particular sequence, for example sorting out the walls of your house before the roof. The same happens in nature.

There are so many incredible and complex organisms, it can sometimes be difficult to imagine how they came to exist at all. In fact, some people use examples from nature to try to say evolution isn't real. The eye is just one example. Because it is so complicated and has so many different working parts, it can be hard to understand how tiny changes over hundreds of millions of years have tweaked and changed not only our eyes, but the way many animals see. The more we look at nature, the more we see wonderful and weird instances of really complicated adaptations that have come about by a series of steps and changes occurring over millions, or sometimes even hundreds of millions, of years. The story of how *Ankylosaurus* got its tail is among them. Now we understand more about the science, we are able to tell much more of the story. Some of this research was done by the North Carolina State University and the North Carolina Museum of Natural Sciences in the USA.

> If I asked you to tell me why the *Ankylosaurus* tail is special, you'd probably say because it had a huge lump at the end used for whacking stuff. But that's only half the answer. Because, if *Ankylosaurus* just had a tail with a huge bony club, then it would injure itself when it was swinging it around. That much weight would be dangerous if the rest of the tail wasn't supported. Imagine your fist as a weapon. Your super fist weapon is made of stone and can bash through walls. Sounds cool, right? Now imagine if you had no bones in your arm. Your magic fist would be almost pointless, because you wouldn't have the power to use it.

When we look at the tail of ankylosaurs, we can see they were not all the same. Not every armoured dinosaur had the big club at the end of a long, strong tail. Using as many fossils as possible, scientists have pieced together how *Ankylosaurus* evolved its deadly tail. If you imagine the tail is like some sort of natural sledgehammer, then there are two parts. The 'hammer' at the end and its 'handle', which is the other part.

As the tail in ankylosaurs evolved, the 'handle' part came first. Like any animal's tail, and your own back, the 'handle' part of the *Ankylosaurus* tail is made up from lots of vertebrae that sit next to each other, each fitting alongside the next. When we look back far enough into the fossil record, we see some of the earliest ankylosaurs, like *Gastonia*, which lived between 139-125 million years ago in North America. *Gastonia* did not have a club and the 'handle' part of the tail was flexible. This long moveable tail would still have been a dangerous weapon. However, moving forward along the fossil record, and looking at more recent ankylosaurs, we find 20-30 million years later, the next step in tail evolution. Around 92 million years ago in China, *Gobisaurus* (go-BE sor-us), another relative of *Ankylosaurus*, showed it had developed a long stiff tail, but still without a heavy club at the end.

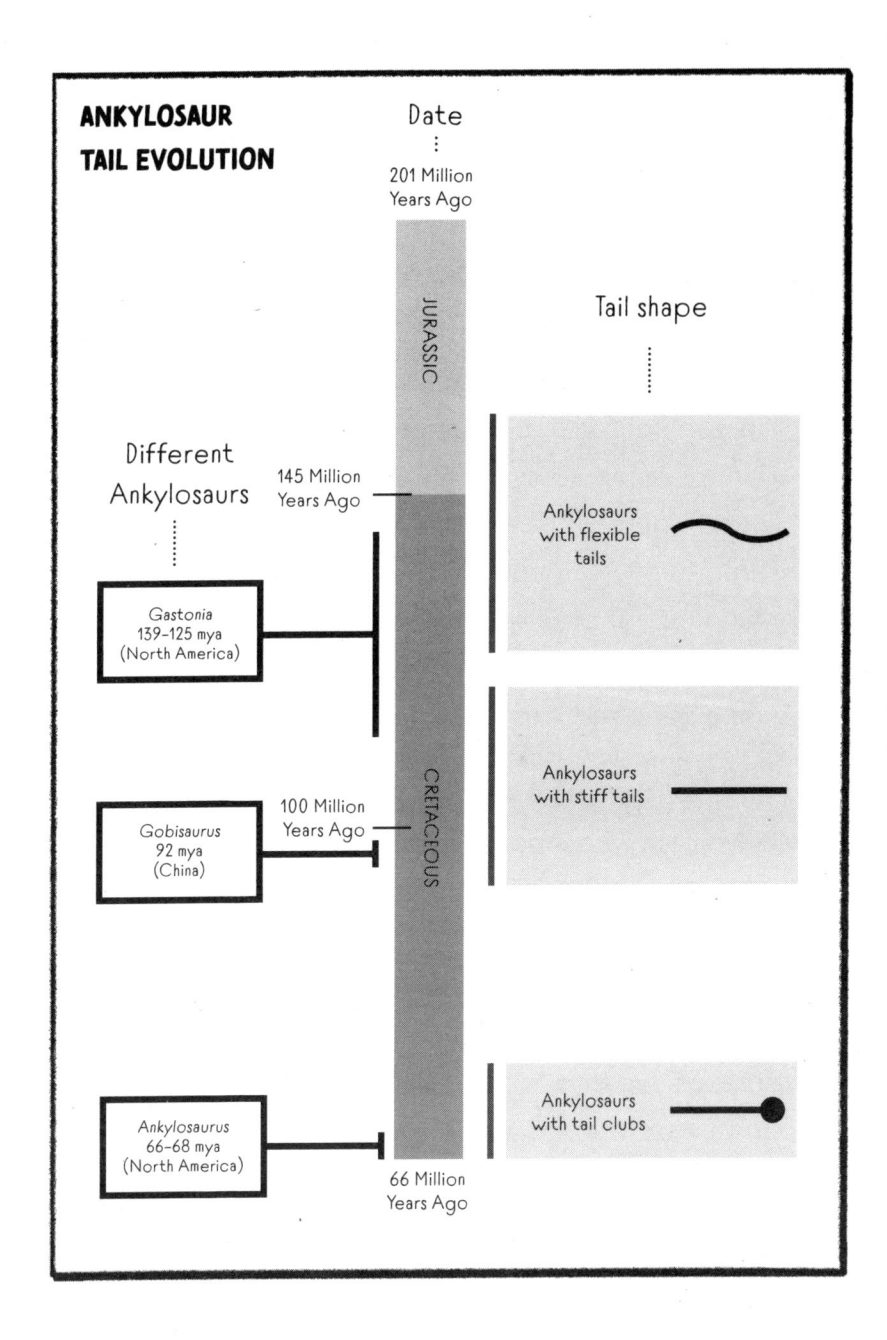

ANKYLOSAUR TAIL EVOLUTION

Date

201 Million Years Ago

JURASSIC

145 Million Years Ago

Tail shape

Different Ankylosaurs

Gastonia
139-125 mya
(North America)

Ankylosaurs with flexible tails

CRETACEOUS

100 Million Years Ago

Gobisaurus
92 mya
(China)

Ankylosaurs with stiff tails

Ankylosaurus
66-68 mya
(North America)

66 Million Years Ago

Ankylosaurs with tail clubs

If you make your hands into two fists and roll them against each other so that your knuckles rock together, this is a little bit like the vertebrae in your back, or in most animals' tails. They fit but they move around too. Now open your hands and link the fingers from your left hand between the fingers of your right hand. You'll notice there is a lot less wiggling about. If the fingers overlap each other by 50 per cent or more, then there is very little movement. Imagine lots of hands linked like this, with fingers on both sides linking into the next one. The same thing happened in the armoured dinosaur tail story, and lots of different species around this time had tails where the individual bones linked by at least 50 per cent. Like our hand experiment, this would have made the tail very stiff.

When we continue looking through the fossil record, we don't start seeing tail clubs until around 75 million years ago, a good 20 million years after the tail became stiff and like a handle. These clubs were made from a special type of bone called osteoderms, which sit up on the surface of the skin, or tucked just underneath it.

By looking at the fossil record and piecing it back together like a prehistoric jigsaw puzzle, we can tell the story of how the armoured dinosaurs evolved their tails. Starting around 125 million years ago, the amazing *Ankylosaurus* tail developed across two major stages over the next 50 million years, meaning by the time we saw the most famous of the armoured dinosaurs, *Ankylosaurus*, it was lucky enough to have a stiffened tail *with* a devastating bone club at the end of it.

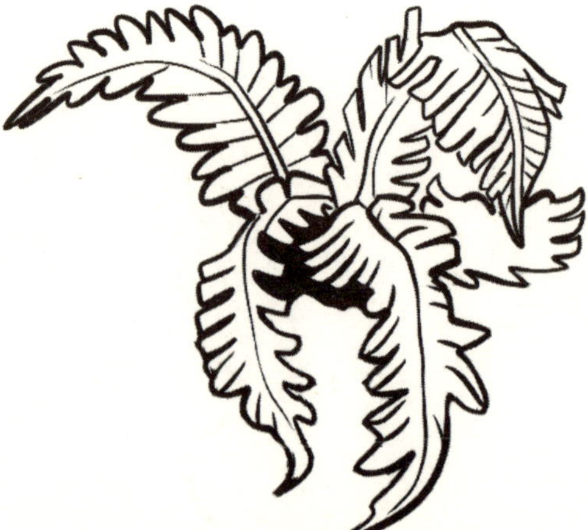

CHAPTER 6
DODGING DINOSAURS

EVOLUTIONARY ARMS RACE

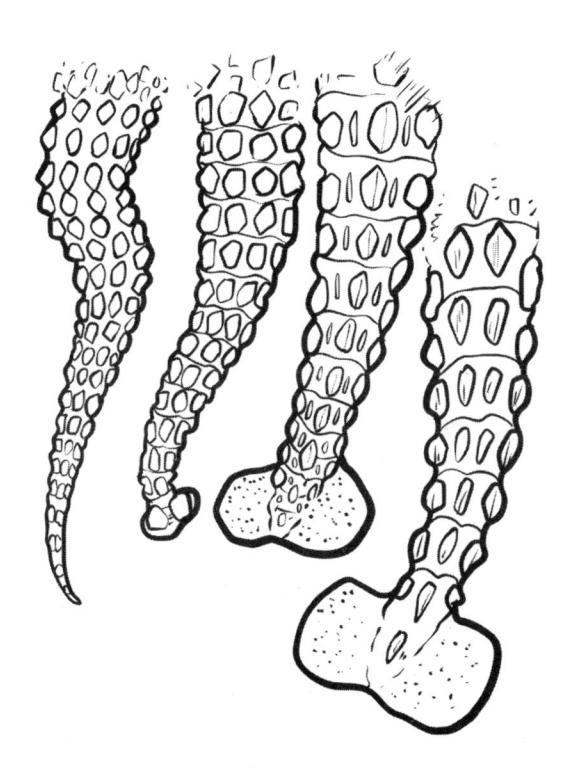

Dodging Dinosaurs

EVOLUTIONARY ARMS RACE

Evolutionary. Arms. Race. Three words you've probably heard before but together they may not make that much sense. First, let's look at a definition for 'evolution'. It's pretty easy. It's the process where we see changes in living things, stretched out over (usually) long periods of time.

Next, 'arms'. No, not the ones attached to your hands. In this case, the word 'arms' means weapons.

And as for 'race', well I'm pretty sure we've all had to join in with a race at some point. Maybe a 100m sprint, or an 'egg and spoon' race.

Put together, an evolutionary arms race is the process we see in nature where different living organisms develop different weapons, and ways to avoid weapons, to beat each other in the race to survive. The only difference is that, unless a group goes extinct, this sort of race doesn't have a finish line. If a cheetah is able to run fast, then maybe a gazelle evolves to twist and turn while running, helping it to avoid its predator. If the cheetah then develops, over millions of years, large nostrils, a short face and special bones to stop itself overheating while running and become a better hunter, maybe a gazelle develops keener eyesight, to enable it to start running sooner, and increase its chances of survival. And on and on it goes.

THE BATTLE

The early morning sun creeps over the horizon and shines into a dense patch of ferns. A cold mist swirls close to the ground. A clump of soft young shoots is pulled up, great steaming breaths break up the misty air. Adding to the noise of the heavy breathing is the sound of teeth tearing leaves, like giant scissors cutting through rough paper. And there's a constant deep rumbling of a huge stomach, working overtime to digest a lot of food.

The ancient *Ankylosaurus* is always awake early. He likes the cold morning air and needs to feed most of the day anyway. He's old and slower than ever, with broken spines and scratches in his armour showing he has spent much of his life fighting to survive. His eyes are cloudy

Dodging Dinosaurs

The Battle

now and his hearing has never been great, but he senses movement not far away and he lifts his tail as a warning to any would-be predators.

Instead, the ferns part and a younger *Ankylosaurus* approaches the old male. The older animal drops his head close to the ground and lifts his deadly tail high, to show off the huge bony club. The young male responds by bellowing loudly and lifts his tail too. They walk side by side, parallel to each other, both swinging their deadly tails, both walking with exaggerated steps, both trying to show the other who is the strongest. If their displays do not work and neither backs down, then they may fight.

The young male lifts his head and makes a deep call, ready to charge, when suddenly the ferns and bushes part again, and a massive snout appears between them. A young *Tyrannosaurus rex* has come to investigate whether she can find breakfast here. She hasn't seen an *Ankylosaurus* before and is unsure how to tackle one, but it doesn't look too difficult.

She moves closer, her striped, feathery coat blending with her surroundings, and the two big herbivores stop their aggressive display and begin to cooperate instead. They move much faster than the young *T. rex* had expected, and turn to face away from her. Both slash their tails at her, and she begins to realise these animals will not make easy meals after all. She tries to move around to avoid those tails, but the two big males simply turn with her, so their tails are always in the way.

She lunges and jumps onto the old male. She perches on his vast, armoured back. She tries a few bites but only manages to snap at his spikes and thick armour. He rocks from side to side, and she jumps off, only narrowly avoiding a swipe from those dangerous tails. Deciding there is most definitely easier prey out there, the young *T. rex* stalks into the ferns, now very wary after her *Ankylosaurus* encounter, and the two males go back to facing each other, displaying again, safe from predators.

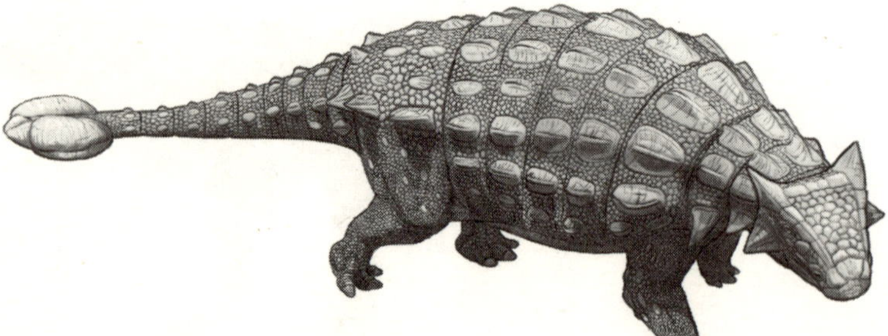

FOSSIL FINDER

PRACTICAL

When I was much younger, I used to love drawing, and at one point, I wanted to be an artist, but then I went down a different path and ended up becoming a scientist. The cool thing is that being a scientist means you can use lots of different skills to explore and understand science, and one of those things, believe it or not, is art. Being able to draw is a useful skill in science and even if you're not good at art, even a basic drawing can help you understand something in science, or allow you to make a more accurate record of what's in front of you.

You might be thinking a photograph is quicker, easier, and better, and besides, most adults at least have a phone handy nowadays. But I'd argue that while a photo is always useful to have, drawing a fossil, or anything in nature, makes you look at what's in front of you. It helps you use those powers of observation, which are like a superpower for scientists. Let's do a quick experiment. Find paper, a pencil and a ruler. Now, think of the biggest shark ever, and draw a megalodon tooth for me. Take as long as you need.

Okay, finished? How does it look? I bet it's a large pointy triangle, with quite a wide base. Am I right? Could be better? This time, ask an adult to find a photo of a megalodon tooth for you on the internet. But before you even pick up your pencil look at the tooth for a minute or so. What's the overall shape? What are the edges like? Which bits are rough, and which bits smooth?

Let's start again, and this time, let's try and make the tooth more accurate. Start with the overall shape. To do this, you use your ruler to draw a line from the top of the page down towards the bottom. This will be your 'midline' ... which will help you make sure the whole thing looks more accurate. Then draw a line near the bottom of that first line. This will help you get the width right.

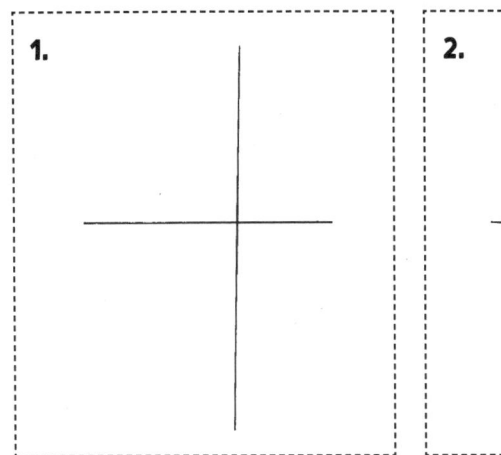

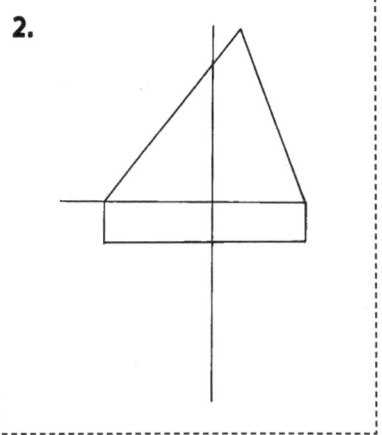

1.

2.

Now, draw the rough outline of your tooth. You'll notice the actual tooth you're drawing isn't perfectly symmetrical. Make sure you get the shape right at this stage, because the next steps come from getting this bit right. You'll notice the bottom isn't straight either. Then start to add some details. Look where the curves, dips and bulges are.

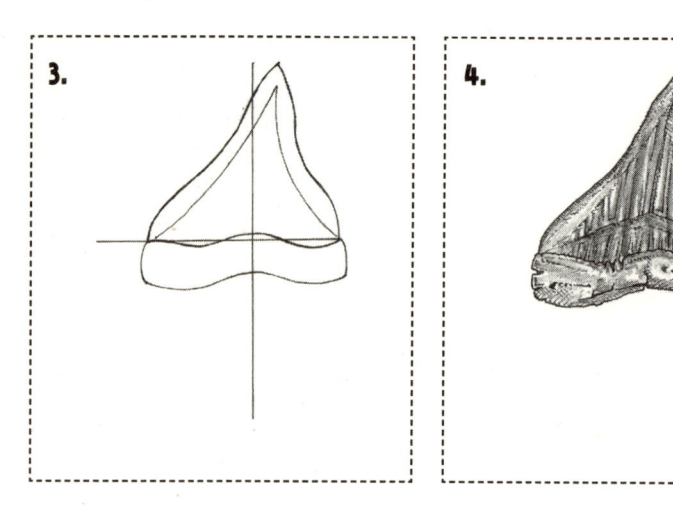

3.

4.

Finally, add in all the little sharp notches to be biting edges, and little holes where blood vessels used to enter. Some of these things can be used to identify species and are really important. Others can be used to make a record of particular fossils.

Being able to make a record of fossils in this way is a useful skill for any scientist. Next time you're in a museum, or find a fossil on the beach, or if you're lucky enough to have a fossil collection at home, start drawing fossils where you can. You'll soon discover that, rather than just looking at the fossils, you're actually beginning to *see* them too.

QUIZ ANSWERS

PAGE 36

How much did *Ankylosaurus* weigh?

Between 4 and 8 tonnes.

Name other dinosaurs who belong to the 'bird-hipped' group of Ornithischia.

Hadrosaurs, stegosaurs, horned dinosaurs.

What covered all armoured dinosaurs' bodies?

Osteoderms – bony armoured plates.

What was special about *Ankylosaurus*?

Its club tail.

What did *Ankylosaurus* measure from the tip of its nose to the tip of its tail?

Up to 8m.

PAGE 74

What was the name of the supercontinent that started to break up towards the end of the Cretaceous?

Laramidia.

How many teeth do scientists believe *Ankylosaurus* had?

More than 71 small, leaf-shaped teeth.

How long is the longest *Ankylosaurus* tail measured so far?

216cm.

Why did a low centre of gravity help *Ankylosaurus*?

Stopped predators from tipping it over to reach its softer body parts.

What did *Ankylosaurus* eat?

Ankylosaurus was a herbivore and ate leaves stripped from plant stems close to the ground.

Jog your memory here

GLOSSARY

Adaptation This can be something physical or a behaviour that makes a species that little bit better suited to its environment. It might be something like a hummingbird having a very light skeleton, making it easier to fly, or a polar bear having a good sense of smell to find food over long distances.

Arms A word that can be used to talk about weapons, from swords and guns, to rockets and missiles. In biology, it can also mean adaptations in the bodies or behaviours of different living things either to make them better predators, or to avoid predators.

Biologist A type of scientist who studies animals, plants, fungi, or any other living thing. Some biologists work in labs, and others in museums. Some work in forests and others in oceans. They study everything from evolution, to DNA, to behaviour.

Cretaceous A geological period in the history of the Earth, after the Jurassic.

Diapsid Means 'two arches'. This group includes crocodiles, lizards, snakes, turtles and dinosaurs.

DNA The simplest way to understand DNA is to think of it like the microscopic ingredients which make up every living (and extinct) thing on the planet. Small changes in DNA can make huge differences in the animals, plants and other living things. We share 98.6 per cent of our DNA with chimpanzees, and roughly 50 per cent of our DNA with bananas.

Femur The 'thigh' bone and usually the longest bone in the body.

Herbivore An animal that survives by eating plants. Animals like zebras, pigeons, hamsters and goldfish are all herbivores.

Jurassic A geological period in the history of the Earth, after the Triassic.

Synapsid Means 'fused arch' and includes mammals and some earlier groups. Synapsids have skulls with a hole behind each eye, which allows strong muscle attachments to the jaw.

Triassic A geological period in the history of the Earth.

Vertebrae (vur-ter BRAY) The back bones in a vertebrate skeleton. Lots of vertebrae together make up the spinal column. A single one of these bones is called a vertebra.

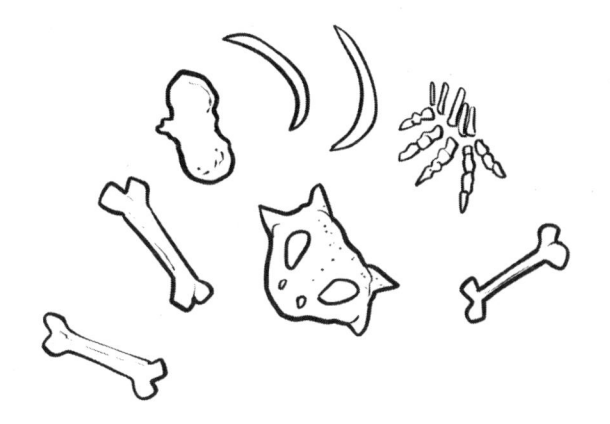

PICTURE CREDITS

Adobestock: 34-35, 80, 85, 89.

Ben Garrod: 93-94 (Drawing a tooth).

Can Stock Photo: 26.

Depositphotos: 16, 17, 18, 19, 29 (elephant), 34, 35, 37-40 (figure), 40 (*Edmontia*), 42, 52, 70-73.

Ethan Kocak: 5, 6, 9, 11, 15, 21, 24, 25, 27, 36, 41, 44, 47, 48, 53, 63, 69, 75, 83, 84, 86-87, 91, 96, 97, 98.

Gabriel Ugueto: 28, 60-61. 64, 65, 66, 90.

Scott Hartman: 2-3, 22-23, 30-31, 54, 56, 58-59.

Shutterstock: 12, 13, 38, 39, 46, 55, 68 & 85, 71 *(Thescelosaurus)*, 76, 77, 92-4, 104 (Stationery).

TheDinoRocker@Deviantart: 20.

Wiki Commons: 37 (*Zuul*).

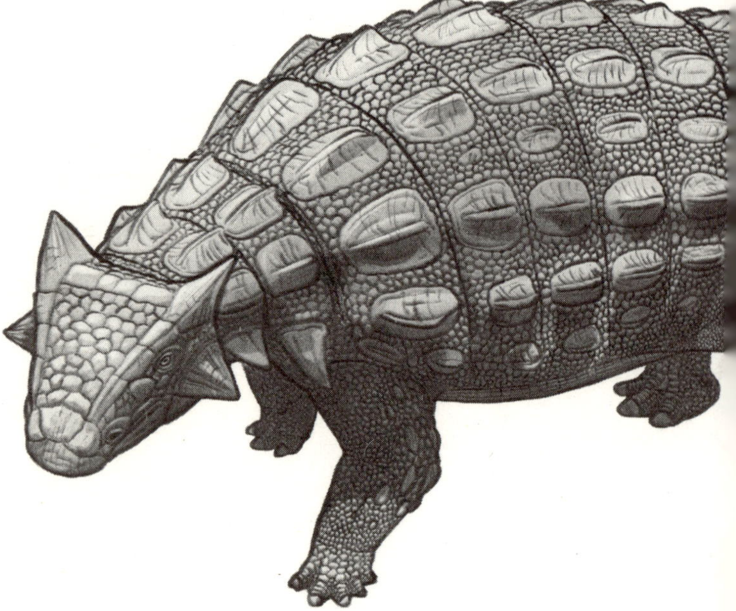

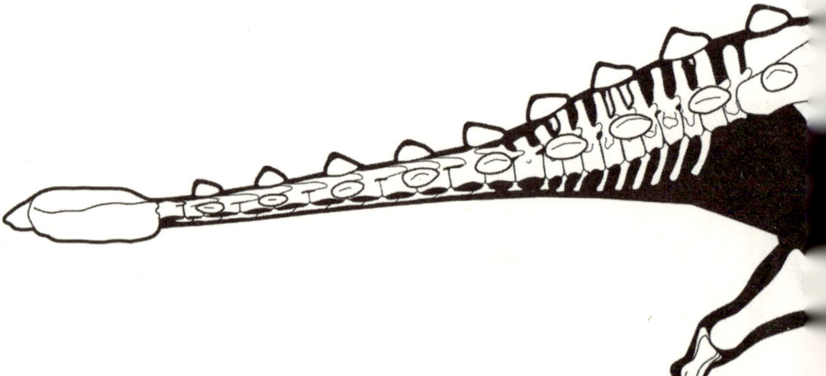

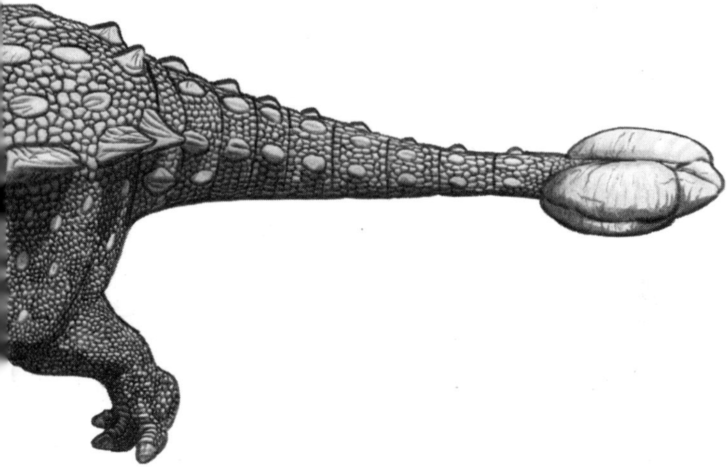

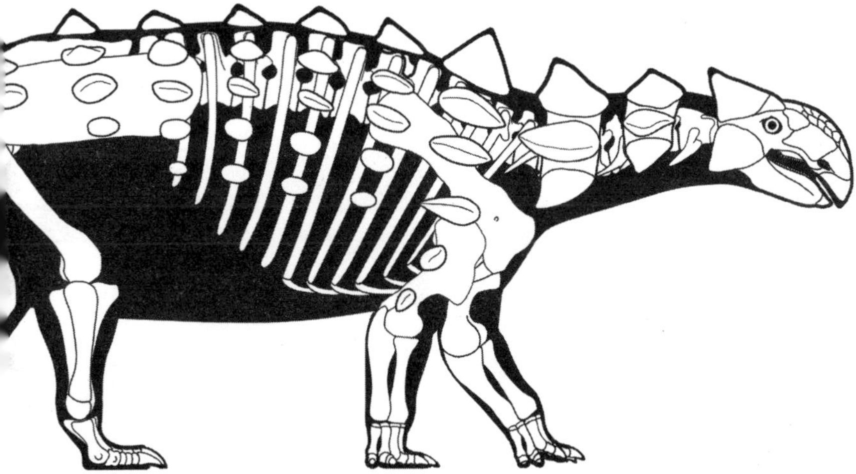

ULTIMATE DINOSAURS
BEN GARROD

DIPLODOCUS

ANKYLOSAURUS

OUT NOW

TYRANNOSAURUS REX

SPINOSAURUS

OUT IN SEPTEMBER

MICRORAPTOR

TRICERATOPS

VELOCIRATPTOR

STEGOSAURUS

COLLECT THEM ALL!

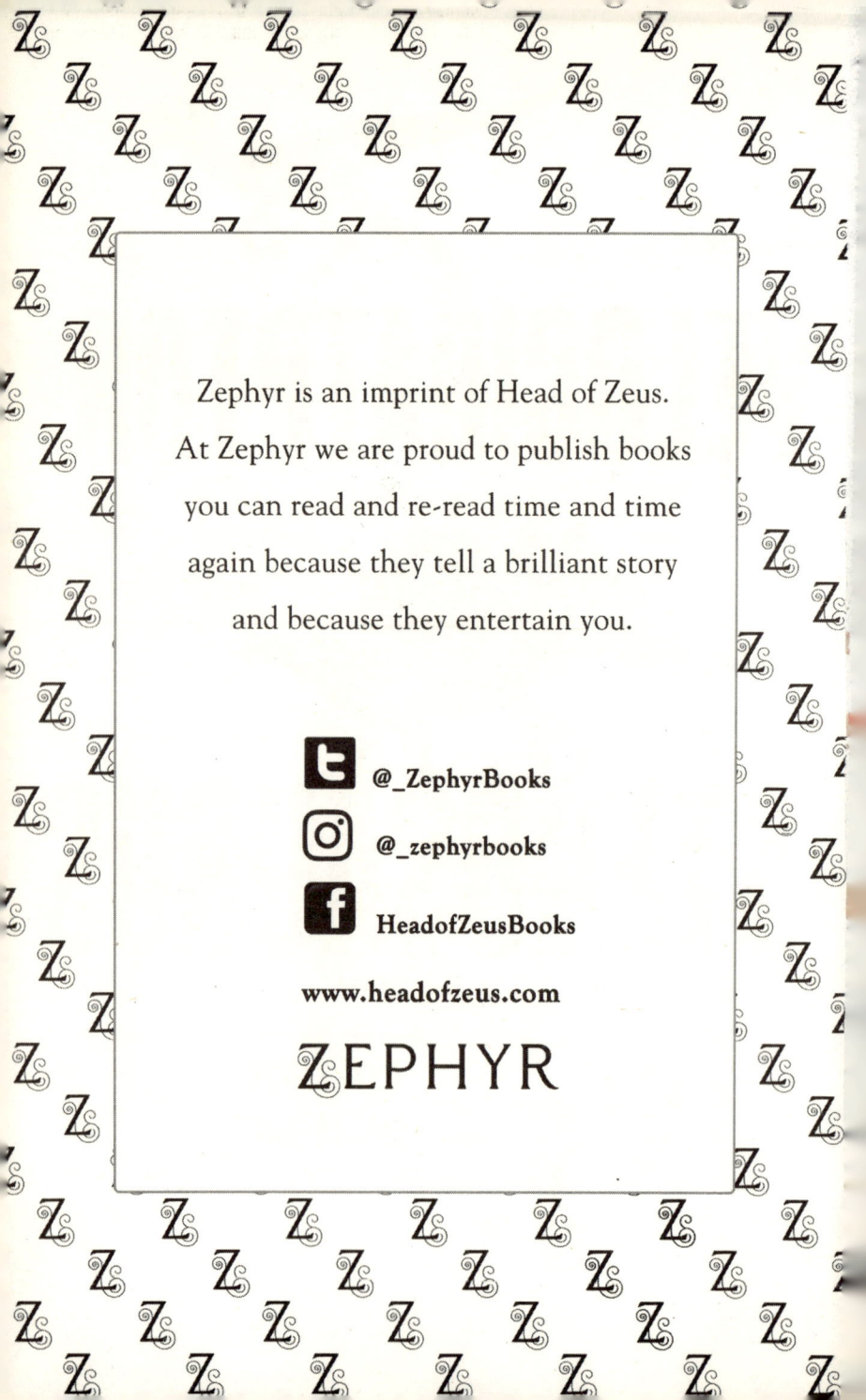

Zephyr is an imprint of Head of Zeus.
At Zephyr we are proud to publish books
you can read and re-read time and time
again because they tell a brilliant story
and because they entertain you.

@_ZephyrBooks

@_zephyrbooks

HeadofZeusBooks

www.headofzeus.com

ZEPHYR